BRENT CROWE

Moments 'til
MIDNIGHT

LifeWay Press®
Nashville, Tennessee

STUDENT MINISTRY PUBLISHING

Ben Trueblood
Director, Student Ministry

John Paul Basham
Manager, Student Ministry Publishing

Karen Daniel
Editorial Team Leader

Drew Dixon
Content Editor

Morgan Hawk
Production Editor

Amy Lyon
Graphic Designer

ISBN: 978-1-5359-3775-7
Item Number: 005810815

Dewey Decimal Classification Number: 248.83
Subject Heading: RELIGION / Christian Ministry / Youth

Printed in the United States of America.

We believe that the Bible has God for its author; salvation for its end; and truth, without any mixture of error, for its matter and that all Scripture is totally true and trustworthy. To review LifeWay's doctrinal guideline, please visit www.lifeway.com/doctrinalguideline.

Unless otherwise noted, all Scripture quotations are taken from the Christian Standard Bible®, Copyright © 2017 by Holman Bible Publishers. Used by permission. Christian Standard Bible® and CSB® are federally registered trademarks of Holman Bible Publishers.

Student Ministry Publishing
LifeWay Resources
One LifeWay Plaza
Nashville, TN 37234

Table of Contents

BRENT CROWE is a thought-provoking visionary and communicator who has a passion to present the life-changing message of the gospel. Brent uses humor and real-life situations to relate to people at the heart of their struggles. The roles of husband, father, minister, evangelist, author, and leader have allowed Brent to influence people from all walks of life throughout his twenty years in ministry.

Engaging issues such as leadership, culture, and change, Brent speaks to hundreds of thousands across the nation and abroad each year and is currently serving as Vice President for Student Leadership University, a program that has trained over one hundred fifty thousand students to commit themselves to excellence.

He is also the author of *Sacred Intent: Maximize the Moments of Your Life*, *Reimagine: What the World Would Look Like If God Got His Way*, and *Chasing Elephants: Wrestling with the Gray Areas of Life*, and is the Associate Editor of IMPACT, The Student Leadership Bible.

The desire of Brent's heart is to see people realize that they have been set apart to the gospel of God and thus, in turn, they must set their lives apart in an effort to capture every moment in worshipful service to Him.

Brent and his wife, Christina, live in Orlando, Florida, with their three children, Gabe, Charis and Mercy. He holds a Doctorate in Philosophy and two masters degrees, a Masters of Divinity in Evangelism and a Masters of Arts in Ethics, from Southeastern Baptist Theological Seminary.

HOW *to* USE

Thank you for allowing this study to serve your group. My hope is you and your students will discover, or rediscover, the glorious journey that makes up this life of following Jesus. To accomplish such an enormous and edifying task we are going to allow one of the greatest lives ever lived to echo down through the ages and speak into our own.

I have been fascinated with the apostle Paul for as long as I can remember. No single person, other than our Savior, has been used to accomplish more of God's purposes. Paul's pilgrimage was filled with every dramatic element necessary for a compelling story: heroic sacrifice, evil villains, uncompromising courage, human violence, battles with nature, friendship and comradery, and finally a martyr's death.

So how can this epic life consumed with cause, purpose, and passion, help us go on a sacred pilgrimage of our own? I hope as you watch, listen, read, study, and converse over the following weeks, something will begin to stir within your heart. I am confident as you progress, you will become convinced to wander well through this broken world—to put one foot in front of the other day after day, until at last we cross over and step into the heaven country. The place where all pilgrims arrive after a lifetime of wandering.

HOW *it* WORKS

VIDEO GUIDE: Begin each session by watching the video of Brent's teaching. There is a Video Guide included for students to follow along while watching.

GROUP DISCUSSION GUIDE: Every session includes a Group Discussion Guide. Allow students time to work through this material and answer the discussion questions.

DAILY DEVOTIONS: Each session, except for Session 8, ends with 4 Daily Devotions. Encourage your group members to set aside time throughout the week leading up to your next group meeting to complete these devotions.

LEADER GUIDE: In the back of this study, there is a Leader Guide to help leaders prepare for each session with Scripture references, optional ice-breakers, key points, and prayer prompts.

Session 1

NOON: COME, LET US WANDER TOGETHER

Start by watching the video for Session 1. As you watch the videos, fill in the following blanks and answer the questions.

- The more we interact with Paul, the clearer the picture becomes of a _____ consumed with his _____.

- We are part of the greatest _____ of all time—we follow _____.

- Paul's was a story that had _____ as its theme and the _____ as the central character.

When grace motivates the pilgrim's journey, four things happen:

1. Grace gives us peace and makes us _____.

2. Grace makes us quick to _____.

3. Grace teaches us how to _____ well.

4. Grace teaches us to _____ completely.

Do you tend to think of yourself as a pilgrim wandering your way home to the heaven country? Why or why not?

Brent said if we deprive ourselves of any sense of pilgrimage, we will miss out on so much of life's purpose. What did he mean by that? What might we miss out on if we fail to see ourselves as pilgrims?

What would you do if you knew you only had 12 hours left to live? Are you satisfied with how you have used the time you have been given so far? Explain.

To journey well, we must embrace the grace of Jesus and let that grace give flavor and direction to every area of our lives. In our first Session we will discover how grace is the foundation of every true pilgrim's journey toward the heaven country.

The Hero's Journey is one of the oldest storytelling devices. The structure of the Hero's Journey has been used for thousands of years to tell all kinds of stories: from Odysseus battling two-headed birds to Luke Skywalker bringing balance to The Force. Something about it resonates within us, because we use story to express things that are built into us by our Creator.

The Hero's journey has three basic stages: The Call to Adventure, the Trials, and the Return.

Think about Frodo's adventure in *The Lord of the Rings*. It begins with Frodo hearing that an overwhelming task has been given to him: to return a dangerous and powerful ring to the fires of Mt. Doom. After his adventure begins, he makes friends who help him overcome the trials set before him by the enemies he discovers along the way. When he finally accomplishes his task, he returns home to the Shire to live happily ever after.

What are your favorite adventure movies?

How do they use the Hero's Journey as the backbone to the story?

Paul was no stranger to the Hero's Journey, because he lived his own. He received a call to adventure on the Road to Damascus in Acts 9. In 2 Corinthians 11:24-27, he outlines a few of the trials he endured on his journey to make the gospel known to the world. And in 2 Timothy, the last letter we have from him, Paul explains that his race has been run, and he is finally headed home.

There is a word used for someone on a journey—a Pilgrim. When a pilgrim is traveling, the land he is traveling through is not his home, but everything he does is for the sake of home. In Paul's case, he was a pilgrim in a foreign land on a mission to take the good news of Jesus to whoever would listen. When his journey ended, he got to go back home.

What's the longest trip you've ever been on?

How did it feel when you got to go back home?

In what ways is the Christian journey like a voyage?

One of the most famous passages in the Bible about faithful pilgrims is Hebrews 11, sometimes called the Hall of Faith. The author of Hebrews listed several faithful pilgrims and then wrote, "These all died in faith, although they had not received the things that were promised. But they saw them from a distance, greeted them, and confessed that they were foreigners and temporary residents on the earth" (Heb. 11:13). In another translation, these people were called "strangers and pilgrims on the earth" (Heb. 11:13, KJV). Consider these four statements about pilgrims:

1. A PILGRIM IS CONSUMED WITH THE UNDERSTANDING THAT HIS/HER LIFE IS ALL ABOUT A JOURNEY OR A PILGRIMAGE.

We are simply temporary residents on earth. Nothing in our lives can or should be separated from our view of Jesus, who has given us this identity.

How does knowing Jesus mean that we are citizens of heaven rather than just citizens of Earth? What's the difference?

What do you think it would look like to live as a citizen of heaven?

2. A PILGRIM IS WILLING TO EXHAUST HIS/HER RESOURCES TO JOURNEY WELL.

If we have established that our identity is that of a pilgrim and all of life happens within the context of a pilgrimage, then it makes sense to use our resources with the journey and the destination in mind. Jesus told us to "store up for yourselves treasures in heaven, where neither moth nor rust destroys, and where thieves don't break in and steal. For where your treasure is, there your heart will be also" (Matt. 6:20-21).

What sorts of things does the world tell us we should treasure?

What things should a citizen of heaven treasure?

How can you treasure those things in your daily life?

3. A PILGRIM BELIEVES ONE JOURNEY CAN CHANGE THE WORLD.

Take a moment to read Hebrews 11:1-12 out loud.

Each of these people was identified as a pilgrim and each of them changed the world. It's not because they were giants or spiritual superheroes, but because they recognized their journey was not about them; it was about filling their role in the story God was crafting to bring the nations back to Him.

List a few things you are involved with on an ongoing basis—sports teams, clubs, friend groups, etc.

How would seeing yourself as a pilgrim on a journey affect the way you interact with each group of people? How would it affect the way you live your everyday life?

4. A PILGRIM LIVES WITH THE TENSION BETWEEN THE PRESENT JOURNEY AND THE DESTINATION.

It's no secret that life is sometimes difficult. Pilgrims live on the rugged road of the redeemed with the knowledge and anticipation of the glorified state that is restoration. In other words, we know there is a real day on God's calendar in which He will make all things new again. And in the meantime, we live and journey through a world where pain, tears, and death are a reality.

How does it change the way you view difficult times to know you are merely a pilgrim passing through?

Living as a pilgrim means seeing yourself humbly. Recognizing that the story is not about you, it's about the journey you are taking at Jesus' request. As we take this eight-week journey together, let's try to do it as pilgrims passing through, learning about the greatest gift that has ever been given to us, and learning how to live the kind of life Jesus envisioned for us when He said, "Go, therefore, and make disciples of all nations" (Matt. 28:19).

As we close this session, take some time to reflect on who you are and what you've been called to do.

What story is your life telling right now?

What story would you like your life to tell?

WHAT DOES IT MEAN TO HAVE A HEAVENLY PERSPECTIVE?

The perspective a story is told from tells you a lot about the story itself. Consider the opening line to the famous book *The Great Gatsby*:

> *In my younger and more vulnerable years my father gave me some advice that I've been turning over in my mind ever since.*[1]

We know a few things just by reading this sentence. We know the narrator is someone we can relate to, and we know he's about to give us a piece of advice. We can reasonably guess he is going to play a part in the story being told: he's using words like "me" and "I," which will continue throughout the story. And since he's a relatable person that is going to play a part in the story, we can assume he is telling us the story after it has already happened.

No matter what comes next, whenever the narrator seems like he is in a tough situation, we know that he makes it through. He lives to tell about it. He already knows the ending, even if we don't. But we do not have his perspective. We have to discover the events of the story one sentence, one paragraph, one page at a time.

You are kind of like the reader of *The Great Gatsby*. You are in the middle of a story you don't know the ending to. But God does. That means no matter what turns your pilgrim's journey takes, you can rest in the understanding that God already knows the ending.

Hebrews 12:2 calls Jesus the "author and finisher of our faith." That means he is like the author of any book you've read—He's in total control of the situation, even when it doesn't look promising for the characters involved. He will always make things work according to His plan.

Living as pilgrims with a heavenly perspective means understanding you are a vessel for God's unfolding story. It is not about you, but you've been given the chance to play a part in getting His story out there for the world to see.

- **When have you faced uncertainty? What was going on, and how did you handle it?**

- **How does it change the way you see uncertain times to know that God is in control?**

- **What role do you play in taking God's story to the world?**

WHAT IS FORGIVENESS? (DON'T BE HELD HOSTAGE BY YOUR PAST)

Forgiveness is a word we hear a lot in church, but it can be a little bit tricky to define. Sometimes it's easiest to understand a word when we put it in a story. As it turns out, Jesus told an excellent story that perfectly illustrates forgiveness for us.

> *"A creditor had two debtors. One owed five hundred denarii, and the other fifty. Since they could not pay it back, he graciously forgave them both. So, which of them will love him more?"* (Luke 7:41-42)

Try to put yourself in the shoes of these people (especially the first person). In those days, the average worker probably made about 300 denarii a year to provide for everything he needed—and this first man owed *five hundred*. He would be in debt for years!

But look what the moneylender did. He forgave the debt. These two people were no longer responsible for paying it back. They wouldn't have to scrounge and save; the debt didn't apply to them anymore.

This is what forgiveness is. If somebody forgives you, it doesn't mean your wrongs are forgotten, it simply means they're not counted against you anymore.

Some of us live with incredible guilt about things we've done. People we've hurt. Mistakes we've made. Sins we've committed.

But as pilgrims on a Christian journey, something amazing has happened to us: Jesus paid the debt we owed because of our sin, and all we have to do is ask for forgiveness. John wrote in 1 John 1:9 that "if we confess our sins, he is faithful and righteous to forgive." Does that mean you forget where you've come from? Absolutely not. What it does mean is that you are walking with fresh legs. You don't have to keep going back to those past sins that have held you hostage for so long because, through the blood of Jesus, God does not count it against you.

- **What is something you need to ask forgiveness from God for?**

- **What has been done to you that you need to forgive someone else for?**

- **How does it affect you knowing that you are forgiven?**

WHAT IS GRACE?

Let's use our imaginations for a second. Pretend that last night you were up all night binge-watching the newest season of your favorite TV show. Because of how excited you were that the new episodes were finally available, you lost track of two things: time (you went to bed way too late) and the fact that you had an important test the next day. So you drag yourself to class and sit with fear and maybe a tinge of regret for staying up so late and completely forgetting to study. You know for a fact you are not prepared, and your grade on this test is going to bring your average too far down to be able to recover easily.

As your teacher is passing out the tests, he stops at your desk and notices your sunken eyes, your exhausted expression, and the worry stretched across your face. "What happened?" he asks.

"I stayed up too late, and I am completely unprepared for this test," you reply with a little bit of shame.

Then your teacher does something incredible. He tells you to come up to his desk after all of the class has their tests and begins taking it. He tells you he's giving you an extension. You can leave early to study, get some sleep, and come back to his office the next day to take the test you should have taken today.

He's just given you grace: a free gift you do not deserve.

God is the master of giving grace, and the finest example of it is when He gave us Jesus to pay for our sins on our behalf. Ephesians 2:8-9 says, "For you are saved by grace through faith, and this is not from yourselves; it is God's gift—not from works, so that no one can boast."

There is nothing you can do to earn grace, and nothing you can do to pay it back. But God's grace is something that should permeate the life of every pilgrim walking their journey back to the heaven country. We have experienced the miraculous grace shown by God, and it is our job to model that for those around us. So they can see a piece of it, too.

- **How has God shown you grace?**

- **How does God's grace motivate you to behave toward others?**

- **How can you best model grace for others this week?**

WHAT DO WE DO WHEN WE DON'T GET WHAT WE ASK FOR?

Try to think of someone in Scripture more sold-out for the cause of Christ than Paul. Go ahead. Try.

Paul met his fair share of difficulties, but his faith persisted throughout all of them. Still, he wrote something interesting in 2 Corinthians 12:7-9:

> *Therefore, so that I would not exalt myself, a thorn in the flesh was given to me, a messenger of Satan to torment me so I would not exalt myself. Concerning this, I pleaded with the Lord three times that it would leave me. But he said to me, "My grace is sufficient for you, for my power is perfected in weakness."*

To be honest, nobody knows exactly what Paul's 'thorn in the flesh' was. Some think it might have been his eyesight, epilepsy, or some other physical condition. Some believe the thorn was a person who was causing chaos and conflict in the church or being especially bothersome to Paul personally.

Whatever the case, we see Paul asking specifically for this thorn to be taken away, and God definitively telling him, "no." Surely if anyone was going to get a free request of God, it would be Paul, right?

Wrong. And Paul knew it—God told him. He said, "My grace is sufficient for you, for power is perfected in weakness." If Paul had it his way, one of those three times he asked God for relief, God would have given it to him. But there was something bigger at work.

As a pilgrim like Paul, you are going to encounter all kinds of things—things you need, things you want removed, things you just plain want. But remember, our journey requires a heavenly perspective. Sometimes, the things we want are not the things God has in store for us. And for a pilgrim, what God wants comes first.

Read Matthew 26:39.

- **What request did Jesus make? Did He get His request?**

- **Why is it a good thing God didn't "let this cup" pass from Jesus?**

- **What is something you've asked for, but not gotten?**

- **Are you more concerned with getting what you want or aligning with God's will?**

- **How do your actions reflect your answer to the previous question?**

Session 2

3PM: LUKE ALONE IS WITH ME

Start by watching the video of Brent's teaching for Session 2. As you watch, interact with the following questions.

Review 1 Timothy 4:11. What does this short verse tell us about Paul's journey?

While Brent shares the story of Edith Wilson Macefield, jot down a list of some of the surprising or remarkable things Macefield did:

-

-

-

-

What impressed or surprised you most about Edith Wilson Macefield?

What can we learn from Macefield's story about what it means to live for Christ during our pilgrim journey?

What role does friendship play in our journey toward the heaven country? What can we learn from Barry's example?

Who stuck by Paul to the very end? What role did friendship play in Paul's journey?

While Paul certainly would have been feeling lonely as the end of his life drew nearer and nearer, he thought about the people who had invested in him and served him. In this moment he confessed his thankfulness that Luke was still with him. While we are called, individually, to follow Jesus, none of us are called to follow Christ on our own. We need the friendship, support, and accountability that can only be found by cultivating intentional relationships with other faithful followers of Jesus.

THE VALUE OF FRIENDSHIP

Making friends is a funny process. You are probably surrounded by people most of your day—in school, in lines at restaurants, at the mall—but for whatever reason, you find a handful of them that make you say, "let's be friends."

Friends are important. They have our backs. They call us out when we need to be kept in check. They listen to us when we're sad and celebrate with us when we're happy.

Who would you consider to be your oldest friend?

What is this person like?

Why do you think you two are friends?

When Paul wrote Timothy in what we believe was his final letter, he said something interesting: "Only Luke is with me" (2 Tim. 4:11).

In his final moments, he was all at once aware that so many people had left him, but at the same time grateful that Luke was faithful to him until the end.

This little sentence about Luke communicates volumes concerning his friendship. Looking back at everything Paul wrote, we get the idea he valued friendship immensely. We watched his friendship with Luke over many years (Acts 16:10, Col. 4:14, Philem. 24). We saw him journey with Barnabas, one of the first to accept Paul's testimony of conversion. And of course, we saw Timothy, whom Paul had befriended and become a spiritual father to from his teenage years until the writing of this letter.

Describe a time someone believed in you. What is your response to knowing someone believes in you?

What is the best way someone can show you they are your friend?

Other friends and companions during his pilgrimage include Priscilla and Aquila, Silas, John Mark, and Titus. After a casual glance at Paul's friendships, the question becomes, what can these individuals teach us about the value and role of friendship?

FRIENDS PRIORITIZE PRESENCE OVER PRODUCTIVITY

In our world, "friend" doesn't quite mean what it used to. So many of our "friendships" are really just acquaintances or associations—someone we have a common interest with or someone we comment back and forth with on Instagram photos.

Paul's idea of friendship was a little bit different. He gives us two ways of looking at friendship in these verses. The first is in 2 Timothy 4:10, and it shows us what friendship does not look like:

> Because Demas has deserted me, since he loved this present world, and has gone to Thessalonica.

When Paul said "deserted," he used a word that means "to abandon, desert, leave in straits, leave helpless, leave in the church, let one down."[1]

Without giving names, when is a time you've felt let down by someone?

Afterward, how did you feel about that person, and how did you handle those feelings of being let down?

Paul wasn't just surrounded by deserters, though. He said something remarkable in the next verse:

> Only Luke is with me. Bring Mark with you, for he is useful to me in the ministry (2 Tim. 4:11).

Paul hit on something important here. Real friends value *being with* over *doing for*. A true friend physically shows up, as opposed to sending some love on social media or shooting a text with a timely GIF. True friends are present. They are fellow pilgrims wandering their way home. They don't just stand on the sidelines and cheer you on; they walk shoulder-to-shoulder with you so you can bear one another's burdens.

What does it mean to be present with someone?

List some distractions we face when trying to be present with the people around us.

How can you be more intentionally present when you're around your friends?

FRIENDS DON'T HAVE TO QUALIFY TO RECEIVE QUALITY

Think about the way people interact with each other these days. Unfortunately, so much of it is fake and based on posturing and an over-concern with appearance. For example, we spend so much time perfecting how we look on social media, always trying to crop out the unwanted and selecting just the right filter. We have become experts at distorting who we are. And sadly, this has affected our approach to friendships.

How do you see people pretending to be someone or something they're not?

Why is it tempting to show the people around us only the good sides of who we are?

Why is it important for our friends to see every side of us—the good and the bad?

At the end of his life, there was little Paul could offer Luke. In fact, it was probably Luke, a doctor, who would have been providing something for Paul—not the other way around. Even when Paul couldn't reciprocate the friendship and love Luke demonstrated for him, Luke gave it anyway. He stuck through to the end. He didn't give up just because Paul couldn't put on a good face for him.

Luke demonstrated a particular kind of love by doing this: *phileo*, or brotherly love. Read C.S. Lewis' words about this kind of love:

> Friendship is something that raised us almost above humanity. This love, free from instinct, free from *all duties but those which love has freely assumed*, almost wholly *free from jealousy*, and free without qualification from the need to be needed, is eminently spiritual [emphasis mine]. It is the sort of love one can imagine between angels.[2]

Look at the italicized phrases in the definition. What do you think are duties that love "has freely assumed"?

Why is it difficult to be free from jealousy?

How should we react when something wonderful happens to or for a friend?

Share about a time when something amazing happened to you and someone responded in love—free from jealousy.

FRIENDS SEEK TO UNDERSTAND BEFORE BEING UNDERSTOOD

As we've seen, Paul was no stranger to struggles. But even though he had more than enough on his plate, he still found time to include this at the beginning of his letter to Timothy:

"Remembering your tears, I long to see you so that I may be filled with joy" (2 Tim. 1:4).

Despite the difficult times he was experiencing, Paul took time at the beginning of his letter to Timothy to say, "Hey, buddy, I know it was really tough on you the last time we had to say goodbye to each other. I know there were a lot of tears shed. I think of you like a son and want you to know I haven't forgotten how difficult this is for you."

Spend the next five minutes trying something out. Break off into groups of two or three and take turns telling each other 1) something good that happened to you this week, and 2) something bad that happened to you this week. After one person talks, the other asks questions about the things he or she just heard. In your groups, seek to understand and *empathize* with what you were just told.

Imagine how different our relationships and friendships would be if we spent more time listening, understanding, and really processing what our friends tell us. As pilgrims on a similar journey, our purpose is not to be heard, but to listen to as many people as we can and form true, real, lasting friendships. The kinds of friendships that are based on sacrifice, respect, and brotherly (or sisterly) love.

Adventure is out there, but sometimes it doesn't look how we imagine it to look. That's why it's important to journey alongside fellow travelers. Everyone journeys; no one should journey alone. To do so would be to miss out on so much of the adventure that is our pilgrimage.

List your closest friends in the space below. Beside the people you listed, write one thing you can do to be a better, truer friend to them. Make a plan to put at least one of these into action this week.

INSECURITY. WHERE DOES OUR SECURITY COME FROM?

If there's one thing our culture is good at, it's making us feel like we're not good enough.

- "You're not skinny enough."
- "You're not strong enough."
- "You're not cool enough."
- "You're not pretty enough."

It's easy to let that get to you. When people say things that affect the way you see yourself, it's tough to shake it. When you compare yourself to someone who seems to have it all together, it's tricky to dig yourself out of the hole comparison puts you in.

The truth is any time we start finding things around us to give us our worth and our identity, we're going to run into this problem. The world has all kinds of competing ideas about what makes someone worthwhile, about what constitutes living a good life, about the kind of human you should be toward the people around you.

Fortunately for us, we don't have to rely on the shifting winds of culture to give us our identity. We don't have to search to figure out who we are. Jesus has given that to us already. In Romans 6:6 and 6:10, Paul describes our new life for us:

> *For we know that our old self was crucified with him so that the body ruled by sin might be done away with, that we should no longer be slaves to sin ... In the same way, count yourselves dead to sin but alive to God in Christ Jesus (Rom. 6:6,10).*

We know what we are dead to sin. We know what we are alive for Christ. And we know what we should look like: the one who raised us back to life with Him.

Our identity shifts from being one dead in sin to one who has been made a new creation by Jesus. So now our identity as pilgrims walking back to our heavenly home is set in looking as much like Him as we can.

- **How does the world seek to define you?**

- **How does Jesus give you a new identity?**

- **What characteristics of Jesus should you adopt?**

SAVED BY GOD FOR SOMETHING, NOT JUST FROM SOMETHING

I know a man who used to be a drug dealer. He spent years of his life trying to get ahead in the world, trying to stack up riches for himself, and searching out every kind of pleasure the world can offer. In that quest, he also almost destroyed himself. He became addicted to the very drugs he was selling. He became hopeless. He lost everything.

And then Jesus saved him, miraculously, in what he called a "Paul-like experience" in his room. He got out of the drug business, got clean, and now has devoted his life to making disciples of Jesus. He says this all the time: "You were not saved *from* something, you were saved *for* something."

Read Acts 9:26-28.

Before Paul's miraculous conversion, he had quite a reputation: he loved ordering the death of Christians. You can imagine what kind of reaction the disciples had in verse 26—they probably thought he was there to kill them.

But here's the thing. When someone truly encounters and follows Jesus, they are made entirely new. Just like the man I mentioned a moment ago, Paul was entirely repurposed. He had a new purpose revealed in Acts 22:21, "He said to me, 'Go, because I will send you far away to the Gentiles.'"

For the rest of Paul's life, he was not just a man saved out of something bad; he was a weapon for God's kingdom who would be instrumental in taking the gospel to people who had never heard of Jesus before. He did not despair over the man he used to be. Instead, he rejoiced in the man God made him into.

You, like Paul, have a purpose. You have not just been saved *from* something, you've been saved *for* something. You are uniquely gifted to do the thing God has called you to do.

- **What has God saved you *from*?**

- **What has God saved you *for*?**

- **Take some time to pray, surrendering yourself to whatever God wants you to do. Record anything you feel Him saying to you in the space below.**

YOUR MISSION, SHOULD YOU CHOOSE TO ACCEPT IT

In 2012, a small team of highly trained military contractors had a very specific mission: protect a building called "The Annex" and any US ambassadors staying at the embassy close by.[3] A diplomat showed up, and this highly trained squad started watching to make sure he was safe.

But soon, everything went wrong. A local military resistance assaulted the embassy with guns and explosives and chaos. The soldiers sprung into action, doing everything they could to keep the diplomat safe.

They were then met with even worse news—backup was not on the way. It was entirely up to them to survive and keep the diplomat—and the embassy—safe. But the more dire the situation became, the more focused they were. They had their mission. They had their instructions. They knew what they had to do.

You, as a believer, are in a similar situation. Read your mission in Matthew 28:18-20.

No matter how chaotic the world around you seems, Jesus' final command is to be your first priority. Go. Make disciples. Teach them to observe everything Jesus commanded. Any questions?

Some of you may be called far away. Some of you may be called to stay home. No matter where you are, no matter what breaks loose around you, your mission doesn't change. You are a representative of the Most High, and it's your job to make disciples of the people around you.

That's what being a pilgrim looks like. You are walking back to your heavenly home, and all along the way you keep doing what Jesus commanded, even when everything feels like chaos. You have your mission, and it won't change.

- **What do you think the life of someone living on mission for God's kingdom looks like?**

- **Is that what your life looks like? Why or why not?**

- **What do you need to focus on so you can live today as someone focused on making disciples for the kingdom of God?**

DOING EVERYTHING FOR THE GLORY OF GOD

"So, whether you eat or drink, or whatever you do, do everything for the glory of God" (1 Cor. 10:31).

At first glance, Paul's instruction in this verse seems simple enough. "Alright, if I'm doing something, I should do it to the glory of God." Got it. Moving on.

But wait just a second. There are some important words in the second half of the sentence: "Whatever you do."

These aren't fancy or complicated instructions. Paul meant exactly what he said. Whatever you're doing, even if it's just eating and drinking, do it to the glory of God.

A pilgrim's life is consumed with the desire to bring glory to God, so it only makes sense that whatever he or she does ultimately works toward that end. Whenever a pilgrim goes to school, plays sports, auditions for a play, meets up with friends on the weekend, tweets, or, well, does anything at all, he or she is looking for ways to bring God glory.

There are probably two different aspects of bringing glory to God that can help us visualize this idea. First, whatever a pilgrim does will be done in a way that pleases Him. Christians should be writing stellar books, composing the most beautiful music, cooking the most delicious food, and forging the most healthy friendships because they serve a God who is excellent—so they, too, will want to be excellent at everything they do.

Second, they will aim to live in a righteous way that causes others to notice how great their God is. When pilgrims' friends look at the way they live—no matter what aspect of their lives are being watched—they see something different. Something otherworldly. They see radical kindness, gentle strength, and joy when the world would think it impossible.

- **Take five minutes to reflect on the various activities you are involved in.**

- **How can you do those things with excellence?**

- **How can you use those things to bring glory to God?**

Session 3

4PM: HEAD IN THE CLOUDS

Start by watching the video of Brent's teaching for Session 3. As you watch the video, complete the following:

List some of the things Brent mentions Paul was able to accomplish during his missionary journeys:

-

-

-

-

The reason Paul was able to stay so focused on journeying well on earth was because he had fully embraced a _____ mindset.

To live effectively on earth and journey well, we must fully _____ heaven's _____ for our lives.

Paul lived with a heavenly mindset, yet his feet were planted firmly on the ground. What did Brent mean by this?

What stands out to you most about Paul's heavenly mindset? How did he balance that mindset with a focus on living for God in the present?

When it comes to living with a heavenly mindset and keeping your feet firmly planted on the ground, which comes more easily to you? Which is more difficult? Explain.

In this session, we will unpack how we might follow Paul's example in keeping our eyes fixed on our heavenly future during our pilgrimage on this earth. As we do so, however, we will see how, like Paul, we are also to live intentionally in the present, making the most of the many opportunities God gives us to impact the world for His kingdom.

There's something to be said for being dressed for the occasion. On the last night of my honeymoon, my wife and I were supposed to get dressed up in what I can only describe as "big church" clothes. While my wife was getting ready in an elegant fashion, I was standing in front of a mirror with a dress shirt on and staring at the tie in my hand without even the faintest idea of how to begin. See, I'd never tied a tie before.

I told her that I had to step out for a minute, then rushed to the hallway hoping to find some last-minute solution to my dilemma. Do you know what I ended up doing? I stopped a short, elderly man in the hallway and asked with desperation, "Sir, I'm on my honeymoon, and I have absolutely no idea how to tie this. Can you help me?" He smiled a little, chuckled, and took me to his room, where he stood behind me on the bed, reached around my neck, and tied it to perfection. Can you imagine?

When I returned to my room a moment later, my wife said, "Well don't you look spiffy in your coat and tie!" I admit, I did feel spiffy—even though I had to have help getting there.

List some situations where it is incredibly important to be dressed appropriately.

Do you play a sport? Do you wear a special uniform or protective gear?

Why is it important for you to wear a specific uniform? What would happen if you didn't?

In Paul's final hours, there is no doubt the theme of his letter to the Colossians was running through his mind: *Christ is enough.* In that same letter, he instructed those who believe to dress a certain way. In Colossians 3:12-14, he said to put on:

> "... *compassion, kindness, humility, gentleness, and patience, bearing with one another and forgiving one another if anyone has a grievance against another. Just as the Lord has forgiven you, so you are also to forgive. Above all, put on love, which is the perfect bond of unity.*"

As we get dressed for our journey as pilgrims, let's take a look at a few elements of the "Wardrobe of Grace."

KINDNESS: HOW WE RELATE TO OTHERS

Kindness is different than compassion, which is more focused on how you feel toward others. Kindness focuses on how we act. You might have compassion on someone who is hurting or struggling, but a pilgrim on his or her journey acts with kindness toward everyone he or she encounters. Kindness has to do with our everyday demeanor.

Sometimes, it's easier to understand what kindness is by getting an idea of what kindness looks like when people show it to us. Imagine the following scenario and spend some time talking about it with your group:

You've just had a really long, difficult day, and your friend wants to cheer you up. Which of these actions would mean the most to you, personally, and why?

A. Coming over to your house, sitting on your floor, and listening to you explain what is wrong.

B. Calling all of your friends and planning an impromptu surprise party, so you can hang out with everybody you love.

C. Giving you space to sit and unwind in private.

D. Inviting you out for a night at the movies to get your mind off it.

Kindness is not limited to situations like this, but is something that should permeate everything about how we interact with others: we should be kind in our relationships, kind on social media, kind when we leave a tip after a meal, and kind when we talk about people we don't even know. Pilgrims act well toward everyone around them.

HUMILITY: HOW WE VIEW OURSELVES

If kindness is easily noticeable, something we wear on the outside and show to others, then humility is kind of the opposite. Paul wrote in Philippians 2:3, "Do nothing out of selfish ambition or conceit, but in humility consider others as more important than yourselves."

We live in a world that doesn't give much consideration to humility. Self-worship is everywhere as people seem to prop themselves up to look perfect from the outside. Instead of drawing attention to him or herself, a humble person will be almost the opposite. A humble person is sometimes difficult to find after a dinner party because he has quietly slipped out to wash the dishes. She may be difficult to spot at church because the spotlight isn't the thing she seeks. Maybe they're the reason the trash is always taken out, even though nobody really knows who does it.

Who is someone in your life you would consider humble?

What do they do that communicates how humble they are?

How does humility emulate, or look like, Christ?

You have a chance to demonstrate Christ to the world by acting kindly and living humbly. You also get the chance to do that by embodying gentleness, which is not an action or an attitude about yourself, but is the attitude you have toward others.

GENTLENESS: OUR ATTITUDE TOWARD OTHERS

One of the easiest ways to think about gentleness is the way Eugene Peterson phrases it in The Message translation: Quiet strength. Someone who is gentle is not weak or wimpy; instead, they respond reasonably and peaceably even when they have the ability to be forceful and overpowering.

Being gentle does not mean being wishy-washy or a pushover; it means you consider your actions and reactions before you act on them. A gentle person is capable of great strength, but chooses to express that strength in appropriate ways for the good of others.

Being gentle does not mean never making demands; it means making proper demands. It doesn't mean having no backbone; it means the opposite. Gentleness is strength under control.

Jesus is the ultimate display of gentleness. He was the Son of God, but He did not wield that power like a weapon to overcome the weak; instead, He harnessed it to make the people around Him stronger, better, and more like Himself.

Explore each of the following passages. What do they tell you about how to behave with gentleness?

- **Proverbs 15:1**

- **John 8:6-11**

- **Matthew 11:28-30**

Gentleness can be a difficult thing to master, because it is the combination of the two things we have already explored: kindness and humility. We have to understand our own strength, and then we have to use wisdom to figure out how to relate with others the way they need to be treated.

When I think of gentleness, I think of a father who works with his hands every day. His hands are calloused and scarred, he is a little rough around the edges, but when he comes home from work, he greets his children in a tumble as they crash into him. When he holds his child's hand with his own, he is more than capable of crushing it— but he doesn't. Because he knows his own strength and he knows the strength he needs to display to make his children feel loved.

This week in your personal study, we are going to build on these three articles in the Wardrobe of Grace by looking at patience, endurance, forgiveness, and love.

As we go into this week, take a moment to reflect:

Which of these three articles of grace is the most difficult for you to put on? Why?

Write yourself a reminder on an index card, a sticky note, or a piece of paper. Hang it on your bathroom mirror, so every day while you are getting dressed, you can remember to put on the Wardrobe of Grace.

The Wardrobe of Grace is one of the most important things for pilgrims on their journey home. Let's dress ourselves in such a way that we are equipped to handle anything the journey throws at us.

PATIENCE: OUR TEMPERAMENT TOWARD OTHERS

Have you ever sat in a long line and found yourself glancing to the front of it, wondering what in the world is taking so long?

You are far from alone in that. There's something inside of us that reacts strongly against having to wait. Our time is valuable, after all! We can't spend it waiting for someone else to get his act together.

Right?

Paul challenged the Colossians to be "strengthened with all power according to [God's] glorious might, so that you may have great endurance and patience" (Col. 1:11). It was important for him to remind the church to put on this crucial piece of the pilgrim's wardrobe.

Patience is tricky because it's only patience when you might not feel like showing it. You might be on the road behind a really slow driver. You might be waiting for someone to make what seems like an easy decision. You might feel like skipping the long part of a reading assignment because it looks difficult.

But we express patience when we say to those people, "He might just be a nervous driver, so he's being cautious," "They're just scared they'll make the wrong decision," "I don't really want to do this, but I'll be better for it in the long run," or "That was hurtful, but they're probably hurting, too."

Patience means not expecting everything to work out in your own timing or the way you envision it—and part of following Christ is trusting His timing instead of yours. It means trusting His justice instead of yours. It means extending patience to people you don't feel like being patient with because He was patient with you first.

- **When was the last time you felt really impatient?**

- **What's something you're waiting for right now?**

- **Who is one person you need to practice being patient with today? How will you do that?**

ENDURANCE: OUR PERSEVERANCE WITH EACH OTHER

People aren't always going to act the way we think they should act. In fact, members of our own communities, small groups, and/or churches will offend us, whether intentionally or unintentionally. We can practice being patient with them—having a gentle and long-suffering attitude—but that doesn't always tell us exactly how we are supposed to respond.

So how *do* we respond when someone hurts us?

Unfortunately, many are answering this question wrongly. If they don't like something in their church or community of believers, they leave or gossip or hold grudges. Sometimes even other believers adopt a take-my-things-and-leave attitude in response to others who have offended them.

The problem with this approach is twofold. First, responding to sinful behavior with more sinful behavior only brings about harm, not health or resolution. Second, the community that is the church isn't bound together by tribal or individual preferences, but by the gospel; we are trophies of grace that have all met at the foot of the cross. If it is God's goodness that has brought us together, how dare we let our preferences or even differences drive us apart?

In the verse we looked at yesterday, Colossians 1:11, Paul told the church to be strengthened so they can have endurance. Later in Colossians 3:13, he uses this same word, but it can be translated "bearing with one another." That means "making allowances for each other's faults."

You are not perfect, and neither is the person next to you. We can be patient by trusting God's timing, but we demonstrate that patience by bearing with each other's faults and clinging to the thing that binds us together: the gospel.

- **Why is it so difficult to "make allowances for each other's faults"?**

- **Who is someone in your life that just feels impossible to get along with?**

- **Write out a game plan for practicing endurance and kindness toward that person this week.**

FORGIVENESS: EXTENDING GRACE TOWARD OTHERS

Imagine you're on a really long treadmill that keeps pushing you backwards. You can walk forwards, but every now and then you get tired and it keeps scooting you back to where you started.

Now pretend that treadmill is your relationship with another person. A friend or a family member, for instance. And that person put spikes on the end of the treadmill. He said something that hurt you, did something that wronged you, figured out a way to drag you down and cause you pain. Now, every time you stop pushing forward, everything always draws you back to that point of pain.

It's tiring for you. You've got to keep walking forward even though everything is always dragging you back to that hurt. You can't get it out of your head—you're always walking away from it, knowing it's back there, or you let yourself get taken back and hurt all over again.

But then you do something important. You walk forward a little bit and build a barrier. Now, whenever the treadmill takes you back, you get stopped before you ever get to the spikes, to that point of pain. You can see it—it's still there—but you don't get hurt by it anymore. Your relationship can move forward, and you don't have to keep returning to the thing that hurts you.

That's forgiveness—not holding something that someone has done to you against them. It's clearing them of the hurt they've caused.

There is only one piece of the pilgrim's wardrobe that Paul couples with specific instructions: "forgiving one another if anyone has a grievance against another. Just as the Lord has forgiven you, so you are also to forgive" (Col. 3:13).

Jesus is the prime example of forgiveness—we fail Him *constantly*, but He not only forgave us, He *died* for it. As we reflect on what Christ has done for us, let's wear forgiveness like a coat, extending it graciously and freely to those around us.

- **How has Jesus forgiven you?**

- **What do you need to forgive someone else of?**

- **What steps will you take this week to extend forgiveness to this person?**

LOVE: THE VIRTUE THAT MAKES ALL OTHERS POSSIBLE

In Colossians 3:14, Paul takes a turn from talking about the wardrobe of a pilgrim and clues us in to the most important piece. The thing that holds everything else together. He says, "Above all, put on love, which is the perfect bond of unity."

Love is a strange thing to talk about nowadays, because it has become so complicated. We "love" that post, or we "love" eating at that restaurant, or we "love it when" someone does something nice for us. We use the word "love" an awful lot, but perhaps rarely when we should.

In the New Testament, there are four kinds of love the writers talk about: two that have to do with friendship, parenting, or family, one that has to do with romantic love, and the one Paul uses here, which is called *agape*. *Agape* is God's kind of love. It means to care for someone in a way that is motivated by the love God demonstrated for us. It's a sacrificial love, a selfless love—it is the kind of love you practice without expecting anything in return.

It's this kind of love, Paul says, that binds the rest of the virtues he mentioned together. It binds all of us together. Because if we love each other, the rest of the wardrobe becomes easy. If you love your brother or sister, you will demonstrate grace, patience, kindness, and forgiveness.

You see, love is not just something you *feel*, it's something you *do*. God demonstrated His love by sending Jesus to die for us. So we demonstrate our love to others, also.

- **What does it mean to truly love somebody?**

- **In your own words, how does love bind the rest of the Wardrobe of Grace together?**

- **Do you find yourself demonstrating love for the people around you? How can you love better?**

Session 4

6PM: FROM TOLERANCE TO TOGETHERNESS

Start by watching the video of Brent's teaching for Session 4. As you watch the videos, fill in the following blanks and answer the questions.

What makes the church of Jesus Christ an unstoppable force?

Because the church has, at its center, the _____ _____ of Jesus Christ, it was an unstoppable force.

Paul was a torch bearer for the _____ in a _____ world.

What was Brent's point in sharing the story about the dolphins?

What can we learn from this example in terms of how we lean on other believers in our pilgrim journey?

God's people are strongest when they are _____.

And when the _____ is our focus, then _____ becomes the fruit.

Have you experienced the togetherness and unity that comes from gospel-focus? Explain.

How can you avoid letting unimportant things divide you from other pilgrims? What is one way you might promote unity in the gospel in your church or youth group this week?

When the gospel is our focus, then togetherness becomes a natural by-product. As we saw in Session 2, no pilgrim is meant to journey toward the heaven country alone. God calls us to journey together, encouraging and supporting one another along the way. In today's session, we will see that we do this by keeping the gospel as our focus and refusing to let our petty differences keep us from journeying well together.

It doesn't take a lot of effort to look around and see how divided our world has become. We have more ways to stay in touch with people than ever before. We have more opportunities to experience different cultures and points of view than any generation before, yet we still seem so divided along political, social, and ideological lines.

Where do you see disunity today?

What are the things that divide us—even citizens of the same country?

Paul's world in the first century was just as divided as ours is today. The little pockets of people all across modern Europe and Asia each had their own cultures, customs, and priorities—and if there's something people are good at, it's not getting along with people who are different.

But Paul had experienced something incredible: a strange, unnatural kind of unity brought by faith in Jesus. Look at how he talked about people in cities that were as different as any could be:

"To all who are in Rome, loved by God, called as saints" (Rom. 1:7a).

"To the church of God at Corinth, to those sanctified in Christ Jesus, called as saints, with all those in every place who call on the name of Jesus Christ our Lord—both their Lord and ours" (1 Cor. 1:2).

"To the church of God at Corinth, with all the saints who are throughout Achaia" (2 Cor. 1:1b).

To the churches of Galatia (Gal. 1:2b).

For Paul, even though Rome, Corinth, Achaia, and Galatia each had their own pockets of people with different values and priorities, he drew on what brought them together: the gospel. No matter where the gospel goes, it pulls people together by uniting them under a banner that is bigger than the flag of their city, state, or country. It makes them citizens of heaven. Take two cultures that at first glance have nothing in common with each other, cover them in the redemptive blood of Jesus, and they are now one.

How does the gospel embrace differences between cultures and allow people to celebrate a common goal?

What is the difference between being a citizen of heaven and being a citizen of the US?

As pilgrims on a journey, we have a new identity. We are citizens of heaven, bought with the price of Jesus' blood. Let's look at three things this kind of unity brings among believers: a new mind, a new mission, and a common goal.

ONE MIND: UNITY OF WILL

When Scripture talks about our "mind," it can also be translated "soul." In the language of the New Testament, the mind is not just the thoughts you think, but the mindset that comes as a result. And your mindset is always going to influence the way you behave.

Let's look at what a mindset is. Imagine there are two people in a car that are faced with the same problem: they're driving in the middle of nowhere when all of a sudden, a tire blows out. They roll to a stop on the side of the road, and there isn't another car around for miles.

The driver and passenger each have a different mindset about this situation. The driver has a defeatist mindset: he is overwhelmed by the problem and easily gives up. The passenger has a growth mindset: she sees every problem as an opportunity to grow.

What would be going through the mind of the driver?

What would be going through the mind of the passenger?

What action do you think each of these people would take as a result of their mindset?

Paul wrote the following to the people in Philippi:

Make my joy complete by thinking the same way, having the same love, united in spirit, intent on one purpose (Phil. 2:2).

Paul wanted the people of Philippi to have the same mindset, because they belonged to the same family. They had been redeemed by the same Savior and changed by the same gospel. They were pilgrims just like he was, on a journey to the same destination, flying the same banner: the death and resurrection of Jesus Christ.

What is the mindset of someone who believes in the gospel? What is ultimately important to them?

How does believing in the gospel affect the way you treat people around you, even if you disagree with them?

ONE MISSION: UNITY IS A TEAM SPORT

I love watching *Mission: Impossible* movies. In those movies, the main characters are always thrown into a situation that is, well, impossible, and they have to band together to somehow, some way, make a plan and save the world from some impending destruction. They can do this because they're on the same team. They are committed to the mission at hand more than they are committed to their own individual safety or comfort.

What kinds of teams—sports teams, debate teams, school teams—are you involved with?

How does being on the same team with someone affect the way you treat him or her?

Whenever Paul writes about working together for the gospel, he uses a word that refers to athletics, meaning believers are teammates with the same goal: the faith that comes from the gospel.

Take a look at what happens when people come together for the gospel:

Read Acts 2:42-46 aloud.

What problems do you think some of these people faced? How did the group solve them?

The church (not just your individual church, but the church as a whole—all believers all over the planet) is most effective when it works together as a unit. With the Wardrobe of Grace as our team jersey and the Messiah as our captain, we are one people working for the same goal.

Part of what that unity looks like is caring for each other. This can be difficult sometimes—not because it's not easy to care for each other, but because it's difficult to admit when we need help.

Do you find it difficult or easy to admit to people you need help?

What is one way your group can help you with something you're struggling with?

ONE OUTCOME: OUR COMMON GOAL

Let's put this as plainly as possible: suffering is part of the Christian life, because it's part of life as a whole. Paul wrote in 2 Timothy 3:12, "In fact, all who want to live a godly life in Christ Jesus will be persecuted." No pilgrimage has ever occurred without difficulty. The road to heaven isn't an amusement park ride you just board and walk off once the ride is over.

But here's the thing. All of these things—disunity and suffering—are combated with the gospel. When you are born again and enter the kingdom of God, you become a fellow pilgrim on the road to your final home, and you have an ocean of pilgrims alongside you.

Read Colossians 1:24-29 aloud.

In your own words, what is the common mission all pilgrims on the Christian journey share?

What role do you, personally, play in accomplishing that mission?

Steadfastly united, there is no limit to the amount of good the church can do in a broken world; disobediently divided we will only end up on the sidelines as a parade of injustices pass us by.

As you close this session, take some time individually and as a group to consider the following questions:

Who is someone you experience disunity with? What do you need to do to fix it?

List any injustices you see in the world around you. What role can you play to see those injustice healed?

What steps do you need to take in order to walk more faithfully as a pilgrim committed to unity among his or her fellow travelers?

LIVING AS CITIZENS OF HEAVEN

Imagine you've been launched in a spaceship to a planet we just found out is inhabited by aliens. They're sending you and a few people as emissaries—or representatives—of Earth. Also, they don't know this, but their planet is only a few years away from being hit by a giant meteor

You're a representative of Earth with a very important message: come back with me and escape what's coming to you.

Of course, the aliens aren't going to believe you at first. You're a strange-looking human who speaks a weird language and doesn't like any of the food they eat. So you live among them for a little bit. Gain their trust. Befriend them. Let them know you're not out to harm them, but rather you want to help them.

They are going to be watching your every move. Everything you do demonstrates you are from somewhere totally different. You talk and eat differently, you walk and dress differently, you have a different set of values than the ones they possess. Slowly, they start trusting you and seeing that, yes, they are in danger, and they have to come back with you to Earth if they want to live.

This little scenario is not so different from a pilgrim's journey. As a Christian, you have been born into God's family. You are a citizen of heaven, not just a citizen of Earth. As such, you probably look different to the people around you. You have a supernatural kind of patience and kindness. You speak truth and stand up to injustice. Most strangely, you keep talking about a man who *died* to save you.

Living as a citizen of heaven is a lifelong habit, not just something you do for a little while or some of the time. As people look at you and notice that something is a little bit different, you have the chance to do something even more miraculous: you get to tell them the best news of all time. That guy who died to save you? He died for them, too.

- **How does being a citizen of heaven look different than being a citizen of the world?**

- **What kinds of behaviors does a citizen of heaven practice?**

- **If people were to look at you, where would they say your home is—in heaven or on earth?**

FELLOW PILGRIMS ARE FAMILY

For some, one of the most relaxing and healing things is coming home after a long day, shutting the door, and sitting in silence to reflect. They get recharged from being alone. But there is a difference between being alone and being lonely. Pilgrims walking a journey back home are not meant to do it alone. We were built for community.

Look at how the disciples gathered together in the days of the early church: "Now all the believers were together and held all things in common" (Acts 2:44).

These were all pilgrims walking the same journey together, leaning on one another for support. As the church grew and spread throughout the world, they settled into groups, setting up churches wherever the gospel went.

We haven't lost this need today. Still, whenever a believer travels in the Middle East, Asia, or Africa, they greet each other with a warm, "Welcome, my brother!" In places like these, even complete strangers are referred to as family when they are bound together by the gospel.

Jesus knew we would need each other when He established His church on earth. He invested the kingdom in the lives of His disciples, who continued what He started and eventually spread the good news about their King all across the world. Is there anything more unifying than the gospel?

Paul offered this charge Philippians 1:27-28:

> Live your life worthy of the gospel of Christ. Then, whether I come and see you or am absent, I will hear about you that you are standing firm in one spirit, in one accord, contending together for the faith of the gospel, not being frightened in any way by your opponents. This is a sign of destruction for them, but of your salvation—and this is from God.

That should be our rallying cry as fellow pilgrims, no matter what corner of the planet we live on—whether it's across the ocean or across the street. We are one mind, one spirit, one family standing firm and walking our way back home.

- **Do you see the kind of unity Paul talked about in Philippians in your church? Why do you say that?**

- **How can you be more unified with the believers in your family? In your church? In your school?**

LIVING WITHOUT FEAR

One of the steps when training a horse is improving their confidence around unexpected surprises. The trainer needs to make sure that if someone is riding the horse and, say, a plastic bag skips across the trail, the horse doesn't get spooked and run off. If left on its own, a horse can be a pretty jumpy animal. If it's an adult, it might not fully panic, but since they are so big and anyone on their back is comparatively small, even small startled reactions can be dangerous. So what the trainer will do is hold the horse by a lead—a rope attached around their head and snout—and slowly introduce it to quick movements with little objects. They'll take the long end of the lead and throw it behind the horse across its back and watch as the horse jerks its head, moves away, and tries to jerk free to get away from the flying object.

As the horse gets comfortable with a lead, the trainer might introduce something else, like a plastic bag tied to the end of a stick. They will flutter it through the air so it is moving fast and making noises, and the horse will do the same thing: it'll be unstable on its feet, rearing its head, and trying to do anything to get away from the flying bag.

But eventually, the horse will learn these little objects cannot hurt them. They'll quit pulling away and quit reacting at all. That way, if they're on a trail with a rider, they're not going to get spooked by little things darting across the path. The horse will stand still, entirely unaffected by things that used to spook them.

Read the last little phrase in the verse we looked at yesterday from Philippians 1:27-28: "not being frightened in any way by your opponents." The word Paul used for "frightened" is exactly the image of a horse not getting spooked, because they know they are safe.[1]

In the Christian life, we will have things that frighten us. Satan is real, the enemy of God, all the saints, and anything that is good. But Paul knew better than to be frightened by them, because he knew who was in his corner: God, and his fellow pilgrims. When we stand together, we don't have to be frightened by the things the enemy throws at us, because the one who strengthens and binds us together is stronger than anyone who could stand against us.

- **What are some ways the enemy would love to see the church divided?**

- **Why is it important to stand firm with your fellow believers even if the situation seems dangerous?**

- **What can you do to strengthen the unity between you and your brothers and sisters in Christ?**

PERSEVERING THROUGH SUFFERING

In his letter to Jewish Christians who had been scattered around the world, James began with some interesting advice:

> *Consider it a great joy, my brothers and sisters, whenever you experience various trials, because you know that the testing of your faith produces endurance. And let endurance have its full effect, so that you may be mature and complete, lacking nothing (Jas. 1:2-4).*

Sometimes it sounds a little counterintuitive to hear that God allows His children to face trials, but He does it for a good reason: to encourage spiritual growth. He wants His children to be steadfast.

Think back to yesterday's example about a horse being slowly introduced to things that scare him. The trainer isn't trying to hurt the horse or make it scared; he's teaching the horse to have no fear. When the horse encounters something that would have spooked it at one time, the trainer wants to make sure the horse can stand confidently without being scared off.

That's sort of what it looks like for us, too. God allows trials, suffering, and difficult things so we learn to lean on Him for support. So we learn to trust Him even when things are out of our control.

James even took it a step further: he said these trials produce steadfastness, which makes us perfect and complete. Of course, he's not talking about being morally perfect or completed the way we will be when we meet Jesus face-to-face, but rather fully equipped to handle anything the enemy can throw at us. We are pilgrims with a way yet to walk. God wants us walking tall, unafraid, and in unity with the pilgrims walking beside us.

- **What do you think James means by "steadfastness"?**

- **How do trials produce steadfastness?**

- **What is a trial you've faced, and how did it make you stronger once you got through it?**

Session 5

7PM: THE SPIRIT OF ALICE ... AND PAUL

Start by watching the video of Brent's teaching for Session 5. As you watch the videos, fill in the following blanks and answer the questions.

If Paul's life teaches us anything, it teaches us this: with God all things are _____.

Make a list of some of the difficulties Paul faced during his own pilgrim journey.

-
-
-
-

How was Paul able to keep going despite all these trials and struggles?

What was Brent's point in sharing about Lewis Carroll's _Through the Looking Glass_?

Do you tend to think of imagination as an important part of the Christian journey? Why or why not?

How might you minimize the many distractions in your life to make room for dreaming about ways you can solve problems and build Christ's kingdom?

Imagination is sadly something we seldom talk about today. Perhaps this is because we always have our phones out checking text messages or updating Instagram. Whatever the reason, today's session will help us recapture the power of imagination in our pilgrimage toward the heaven country.

It's difficult to think of impossible things. Just try it for a second:

- Try thinking of a color you've never seen.
- Try thinking of an animal that doesn't exist.
- Try thinking of a purely meaningless word.

Human brains don't do well with impossibilities. It's even more difficult when we are involved with so many things that take away our imagination. Think about a regular day. How much time is spent decorating a selfie, playing a game on a screen, or binge-watching episodes of a TV show? While none of these things are bad in and of themselves, we have become a society that is thirsty for imagination, even if we don't realize it.

> **Take a minute to try a group exercise. Start with someone in the room and go around the circle creating a story one sentence at a time. Make it up as you go. Use your imaginations to put the character in your story in all kinds of impossible situations, and then use your imaginations to also get that character out of them.**

Later this week, you're going to dive into this passage of Scripture and figure out just how incredible it is. But first read Paul's words from Philippians 4:13 and let it sink in:

> *I am able to do all things through him who strengthens me.*

Our God is a God who is not daunted by impossibility, and Paul knew this. There were countless times he should have been dead or out of commission—he'd been shipwrecked, beaten, imprisoned, threatened with violent storms, bitten by venomous snakes, and forsaken by his friends—but he was sustained by God for a reason: because God accomplishes His will through His people.

As a pilgrim, you are one of these people, and you are part of a new breed of thinkers. Let's figure out together just what that new breed has that the people around them don't.

UNSHAKABLE BELIEF

Through everything Paul experienced, he held fast to something amazing: God had called him, and would use him to accomplish His purposes.

Read the following passages aloud:

- **Acts 9:15,20**
- **Romans 1:1,5**
- **Ephesians 3:7**

After reading these, take a short break with pen and paper. If you had to tell someone what God has called you to be, what would you say? Write out a short description of what God has called you to do, like Paul did.

Paul knew he'd been singled out, and that God had called him to advance His kingdom. He had never led a movement. He had never planted a church or gone on a missionary journey. He had never been imprisoned or beaten for his beliefs. But God doesn't wait for someone's resume to be perfect before He calls them to advance His kingdom. He specializes in qualifying the called, not calling the qualified.

Who is someone in your life you'd consider to be a "spiritual giant"? What is it about him or her that makes you think that?

Be honest—do you *feel* like God can use you the same way He uses the person you described?

I hope you were honest, because I'm about to be honest, too: I have no doubt that every one of you could be added to the growing list of unlikely suspects, like Paul, God uses to demonstrate His sufficiency.

I also have to be honest about this: feelings are overrated. It doesn't matter whether you feel like God can use you. He can. You just have to learn to believe it. As soon as you believe that, there is no shortage of ways you will be used by God to grow His kingdom.

What is the difference between *feeling* and *belief*?

Why is it so much easier to feel incapable than it is to believe you are capable?

Here's why you should believe that God can use you: because you have been given a specific set of skills and gifts that nobody around you possesses.

SACRED GIFTING

Paul believed that God in His infinite wisdom has given each person talents or gifts:

Now as we have many parts in one body, and all the parts do not have the same function, in the same way we who are many are one body in Christ and individually members of one another. According to the grace given to us, we have different gifts: If prophecy, use it according to the proportion of one's faith; if service, use it in service; if teaching, in teaching; if exhorting, in exhortation; giving, with generosity; leading, with diligence; showing mercy, with cheerfulness (Rom. 12:4-8).

Go through the previous passage with a pen and circle all of the gifts Paul mentioned. Do any of those come naturally to you? Which, and how do you know?

A gift God has given you isn't for your benefit, but is for the purpose of the people you'll encounter on your journey. The body of Christ, or the church, is called a body because the body has many different parts, all of which are used for different purposes. In a body, an arm or a leg has a different function than a liver or an ear—but each of them is used for the same ultimate reason: the healthy functioning of the body it's a part of.

Read the following short list of areas of spiritual giftedness. Which of these seems most like you, and why?

APOSTLE/ MISSIONARY	You will go anywhere at any time to any place God calls you.
PROPHET	You're not afraid to tell people what is right or wrong in God's eyes.
EVANGELIST	You can talk about Jesus any time, anywhere.
PASTOR/TEACHER	You have a strong desire to see people grow in God's Word.
ENCOURAGER	You sense when someone is down and want to help them out of it.
MESSENGER OF WISDOM	You're great in a crisis situation and generally know the right things to say.
SERVER	You have a knack for knowing when something needs to get done, and you do it.
GIVER	You sense other people's needs and figure out how to help them.
LEADER	You are good at getting people to work together for a common goal.
DISCERNER	You can tell when someone is being dishonest, and can figure out what the truth is even when it's difficult.

Everyone is different because God made everyone unique. And as pilgrims, you must keep your eyes on the goal so you can use what God has given you to grow His kingdom.

UNWAVERINGLY FOCUSED

It's safe to say that Paul had a laser-like focus on God's power, and he didn't waver from that focus even up to the end of his life. Whether it was a meal or a missionary journey, packing for a trip or planting a church, listening to the waves hit the boat or writing a letter to the saints, Paul demonstrated focus.

In what ways are you easily distracted?

When you have to buckle down and get to work, how do you make sure you stay focused on the task at hand?

There are all kinds of ways that people try to avoid distractions. They might fast from their phones for an hour a day or limit social media usage. These ideas and hundreds like them may be well intentioned, but if you are focused only on following a set of rules, we create a life of nothing but guidelines. Guidelines are fine for raising kids, but are not necessarily useful for producing mature faith.

Read 1 Thessalonians 5:15-22 and 1 Corinthians 10:31 aloud.

Paul wasn't necessarily focused on staying out of the "gutters" on either side of the lane; he was, instead, intently focused on his end goal: bringing God glory. Instead of focusing on all of the things he should avoid, he kept his eyes fixed on the prize.

What is the primary focus of your life?

What do you need to do to fix your eyes only on Christ?

How will maintaining that focus keep you from falling into distractions along your journey?

What steps can you take to make sure you wake up every day ready to look to Christ alone?

PHILIPPIANS 4:13

If there's one thing you're almost guaranteed to see at a sporting event, it's someone saying they can do all things through Christ, who gives them strength—the implication, of course, being that they are perfectly capable of winning the game because it's Christ who empowers them. Let's take a look at this verse in its context:

> *I rejoiced in the Lord greatly because once again you renewed your care for me. You were, in fact, concerned about me but lacked the opportunity to show it. I don't say this out of need, for I have learned to be content in whatever circumstances I find myself. I know both how to make do with little, and I know how to make do with a lot. In any and all circumstances I have learned the secret of being content—whether well fed or hungry, whether in abundance or in need. I am able to do all things through him who strengthens me (Phil. 4:10-13).*

One of the first things you might notice about this is that the famous verse 13 comes at the end of a section talking about something incredibly specific: contentment.

Being content is less a talent than a skill, and Paul had learned it. He knew how to have plenty and he knew how to have little; he knew how to be lowly and he knew what it was like to have it all—and the kicker is that none of it was about him.

For Paul, it wasn't about how much or how little he had. It wasn't about how well off he was or how dangerous his situation. He was doing everything for the sake of telling the world about Christ and raising up disciples who could continue to do what he did after his journey ended. He was on Jesus' mission, and it was Jesus who was empowering him to complete the mission—that meant he had the strength to be content no matter what came his way ... even if it was prison and his eventual death.

- **What does it mean to you to be "content in all things"?**

- **How does understanding that you are a pilgrim on a journey help you to find contentment?**

- **How does Christ strengthen you to endure both the good and the bad things for the sake of His mission?**

2 CORINTHIANS 12:9—BOASTING IN WEAKNESS

Maybe you have a friend like one I have. I sort of hope you do. Let me describe him to you.

I have some friends who are incredibly supportive, who are quick to rejoice when things go well and quick to help pick me up when they don't. But I have this one friend—one of my best friends in the whole world—who is always the first to speak up after all of the congratulations come in and say, "You could've done that better."

At first this seems like he's just being mean or overly critical, but both of us know his intention is far from that. He's always there to make sure I don't get conceited—to make sure my head doesn't get too big. He wants to keep me humble, and I've given him permission to do so.

Paul had someone like that, too, but his situation felt a little bit different. He was suffering, not being spoken to by a friend. But when he asked God to take this suffering away, this is what God told him:

> *"My grace is sufficient for you, for my power is perfected in weakness." Therefore, I will most gladly boast all the more about my weaknesses, so that Christ's power may reside in me (2 Cor. 12:9).*

Even though this outside force was oppressing Paul, he didn't let it get him down, because it caused him to rely on the Lord even more—and when we rely on the Lord to do what He has called us to do, we will find ourselves in a healthy place. Even if it's difficult. Even if it's frustrating.

A pilgrim will prioritize the mission and his home kingdom above the comfort of his present situation. There will be times when you are tired and worn out, exhausted and beat-up. And then you have two options: you can wallow in your misery, or you can remember, "my strength doesn't come from myself, anyway. It comes from Christ, alone!"

There is no better place to be than living in the power provided only by Jesus.

- **What is something you feel called by God to do?**

- **When have you felt too weary to continue? How did you get past that feeling?**

- **How can you "boast in your weakness" so that Christ can be exalted today?**

EPHESIANS 3:16—STRENGTH THROUGH THE SPIRIT

I hate to break it to you: you're going to have bad days.

It is going to feel like the weight of the entire world is resting on your shoulders. Like every bad thing happens all at once. Some days are like being in a boxing ring with a professional boxer who has you up against the ropes and the hits just keep coming. Days like these are just a part of a pilgrim's journey.

In your Bible, read the prayer Paul wrote for the church at Ephesus in Ephesians 3:14-19.

Paul knew there were going to be days like this, because he felt them, too. He had just finished writing about them! The verse just before this talked about the sufferings Paul had endured on their behalf.

The very nature of Paul's journey required that he rely on Christ's strength as not just helpful, but *necessary* for him to endure and run his race well. You might not be shipwrecked on an island in the middle of a storm, but you *do* live in the middle of all kinds of struggles. Perhaps you have family issues that have been getting worse each year. Maybe you are very sick. You might feel deserted or lost or hopeless.

That's okay, because Paul's prayer for the Ephesians goes for you, too—I pray that you are strengthened with the power of the Holy Spirit, who lives inside of every person who professes Jesus as Lord.

No matter your situation, Jesus is stronger. No matter your struggle, Jesus is Lord. No matter your pain, Jesus is your strength. No matter how difficult a day you have coming up, Jesus gave Himself up for you and gave you His spirit so you could have the strength to endure for His sake.

Take five minutes right now and spend it in prayer:

- **Praise God for being who He is. Name some of His qualities that astound you. Confess the times you have fallen short of His standard and ask for forgiveness. Thank Him for the gift of salvation in Jesus. For giving you the Holy Spirit. For blessing you richly. Pray for the strength to follow Him, no matter how difficult it may be some days.**

1 THESSALONIANS 5:15-22—A NEW BREED

Some of the most popular movies of all time are the *Jurassic Park* movies. What's not to love about seeing massive dinosaurs and following the adventures of those who have to survive when everything goes wrong?

Something interesting always happens whenever there's a new *Jurassic Park* movie: the situations only get more intense. At first, all of the dinosaurs are only on one island. Then we find out they have spread. Eventually, scientists start tinkering around and building newer, bigger, faster dinosaurs, creating entire new species of dinosaurs that are similar to previous dinosaurs, but are better and more powerful in every way.

When we become children of God, He makes us new. In 2 Corinthians 5:17, we learn that as the old passes away, we become new creations when we are in Christ. It's almost like we're a new species of human. Look at something that we, members of this new species of people, have the ability to do:

> *Rejoice always, pray constantly, give thanks in everything; for this is God's will for you in Christ Jesus (1 Thess. 5:16-18).*

For those of us who have been made new in Christ, we don't see the world the way we used to. We can rejoice when things get difficult. We can have an ongoing conversation with the Creator of the universe. When something happens to us that would ordinarily cause despair, we can do the opposite: *give thanks.* This is not average, everyday human stuff; this is divine. It's the stuff of a new species of thinkers: pilgrims on a journey home.

- **How has Jesus made you new?**

- **What are you facing today that you need to approach as a new species of thinker—someone made new by Jesus?**

- **List three things you can give thanks for right now.**

Session 6

9PM: GRACE DEMANDS MORE

Start by watching the video of Brent's teaching for Session 6. As you watch the videos, fill in the following blanks and answer the questions.

Grace demanded _____ of Paul, never _____.

What role does excellence play in the pilgrim's journey?

You can't put a price on a life _____ lived.

How did Brent's story of his grandmother encourage or challenge you?

How is Jesus telling a new story, a better story with your life?

You have the chance to tell a story with your life—a story that has _____ as its theme and the _____ as its central character.

How might realizing that God's grace demands more of us, never less, help us in our journey toward the heaven country?

What might God's grace be demanding of you in the current stage of your pilgrim journey?

Given that we are saved by grace through faith and not by works (Eph. 2:8-9), it would be easy to fall into the trap of thinking this means God has relaxed the standards on what He expects of us. In this session, we will see the opposite is actually the case. If God has truly saved us by grace, then there is nothing He cannot ask of us.

It is Paul's nine o'clock. The end is drawing near. This is certainly not the first nine o'clock hour Paul has spent in the darkness of a prison or dungeon. But this time is different, because this time will be the last.

Imagine you were sitting in your final hour, thinking back over the life you've lived up until this point, and you had the chance to give one piece of advice to one of your closest friends. What would you say?

Paul wanted to make sure he passed something specific on to Timothy, his spiritual son:

Be diligent to present yourself to God as one approved, a worker who doesn't need to be ashamed, correctly teaching the word of truth (2 Tim. 2:15).

This is actually a theme he touched on in most of his letters, because it was incredibly important to him. He wanted every believer to live a life of excellence.

Read the following passages aloud:

- **Philippians 1:9-10**
- **Philippians 4:8**
- **Colossians 3:23**

What do each of these passages say about excellence?

What does it mean to you to live a life of excellence?

EXCELLENCE IS A STANDARD ROOTED IN OUR UNDERSTANDING OF GOD

Excellence is more than just a goal of our journey, it is our standard for how we make the journey. And for pilgrims who are members of the kingdom of God, that standard begins and ends with God, Himself. We can know what God's standard of excellence is by seeing what God has revealed about Himself in Scripture.

We matter so much to God that He paid off our sin debt. He purchased us from the death we surely deserved because of our sin. This is an idea we call grace: a free gift we do not deserve and could never pay back. This is something Paul understood fully: Grace demands more, never less. A right understanding of grace should lead me to lay the entirety of my life as an offering at Jesus' feet.

When has someone done something kind for you?

What has God done for you, personally?

What kind of response should you have to that gift?

A scholar named Andreas Kostenberger said this about excellence:

> *God is the grounds of all true excellence.* He is the one who fills any definition of excellence with meaning, and he is the reason why we cannot be content with lackluster mediocrity, halfhearted effort, or substandard scholarship ... Without God as our starting point and continual frame of reference, our discussion of excellence would be hopelessly inadequate.[1]

What does it look like for us to model God's excellence in our lives:

- **At home?**

- **At school?**

- **Among friends?**

EXCELLENCE IS A DECISION AND AN ACHIEVEMENT

With God as our starting point, we have to take a close look at the things we do. Acting with excellence is about continually aiming for the standard that pleases God.

Once you begin striving for excellence in everything you do, you might notice some changes about yourself. You might notice you develop a low tolerance for doing things half-heartedly. You might see being average as something other people are content with, but you are not. Behaving with and striving for excellence gives you an appetite you never even knew you could have.

Read over the following scenarios and see if you can determine the best response:

- **You waited in line for 20 minutes at the cafeteria on the one day a year they serve your favorite food. When you reach the front, the man behind the counter tells you they just ran out.**

- **You are working on a group project, but as much as you try, they just don't seem to be pulling their weight.**

- **Your teacher starts walking around the room to collect a paper due today, which you completely forgot about.**

Don't mistake our response to grace—living with excellence—as a call to make excellence, itself, an idol. All this means is that with God, our starting point is excellence, and we continually seek the highest good in any possible situation we are put in. This means the student in band practices daily, hits all the right notes when she needs to, and rests when she doesn't. The football player who didn't make the starting lineup doesn't sulk through the season, but continues to practice and serve his team anyway.

What is something you're involved in where you play a specific role—whether it's in marching band, stage crew, a sports team, or even as a big brother or sister?

What does it look like for you to behave with excellence in that role?

When it comes down to it, we seek to achieve the highest good, a standard of excellence, because we are grateful God gave the greatest good He could ever give to humanity: Jesus.

EXCELLENCE IS SUBSTANCE OVER SHADOW

Excellence is not a showy thing. It's not as simple as cropping out the unwanted or selecting just the right filter. In other words, excellence is not fake. Pretend excellence is just a shadow of the real thing, and shadows are not substantive.

Pretend excellence is kind of a dangerous thing when you think about it. It creates a false impression, invites people to trust in something that isn't substantial, and ultimately expresses to God, "I want the greatest good you can give me, but you can't have my highest good as an offering in response."

Why is it so tempting to want to fake excellence rather than striving for the real thing?

How can you tell the difference between fake and real excellence?

Why is pretending to be excellent, rather than actually being excellent, insulting to God?

My hope for all of us is that the joy of the Lord would so fill our hearts that we would be a people of substance. That we would journey well because we have been loved well by God. That our appearances are authentic, not pretend. After all, that is how you know you are a person of substance: when the outward appearance is a reflection of an inward reality.

A CHARGE TO BE EXCELLENT

We are pilgrims on a journey. This means:
- We are wanderers saved by a miraculous act of grace from our Creator.
- We are faithful servants because we've been served faithfully by Jesus.
- We are a people of action.
- We set goals.
- We dream dreams.
- We do not waste the moments at hand, because they will never be here again.
- We are clothed in grace and humility toward the people around us, no matter how they treat us.
- We are entirely motivated by love.

As we wander this world as pilgrims making our way home, let's walk in a way that models excellence. We don't do it to check a box or earn favor from God, but we do it out of an overflow of gratitude for the grace that has been given to us. If we take this seriously, we can be living, breathing examples to an unbelieving world of our perfect, excellent, gracious Creator.

Think back to the hypothetical situations we talked about a few minutes ago. It can be easy to imagine excellent responses to imaginary scenarios, but it's a little more difficult to put them into practice in our daily lives. Spend some time thinking about the following prompts and record your answers.

- **The person you are closest with:**

- **The person it's most difficult for you to get along with:**

- **A difficult situation you're facing:**

Now go back and explain how you can act with excellence toward each individual this week.

LIVING WITH PURITY

The first time Paul wrote Timothy, he gave him some important advice:

> *Don't let anyone despise your youth, but set an example for the believers in speech, in conduct, in love, in faith, and in purity. Until I come, give your attention to public reading, exhortation, and teaching (1 Tim. 4:12-13).*

Even though Timothy was young, Paul knew he could be the example his church needed to see. His youth did not disqualify him from modeling the kind of behavior the whole church should practice. One of those areas is in purity.

We test the purity of things all the time. One of the most important things we test is water. Testing the purity of water means taking a sample and seeing how much extra stuff is in it. Water testers look for chlorine, nitrates, and minerals, and compare it to what we know to be safe drinking levels. If water is pure, it is clean. It doesn't have harmful chemicals or impurities that would cause problems for the people drinking it.

In the same way, Paul wanted to remind Timothy to remain pure. To not be tainted by the impurities of the world, to be motivated by love and unity, to remain true to the gospel he had been entrusted with. We have the same calling today. We are surrounded by worldly influences that threaten to ruin our witness, damage our reputation, and damage our relationship with the Lord.

Living with purity is a daily task. It means waking up every day and deciding to chase the things of God rather than the influences of the world. It means acknowledging the desire of the flesh but moving away from it, so we can stand as an example of upright living in front of the people looking on, whether they are believers or unbelievers.

- **What do you think it means to be pure?**

- **List a few things the world offers that are impure.**

- **What steps do you need to take to walk in purity?**

LIVING WITH HOLINESS

In Ephesians 1:4, Paul wrote, "For he chose us in him, before the foundation of the world, to be holy and blameless in love before him."

"Blameless" is a word we don't have much trouble understanding. If you are blameless, you've done nothing wrong. You have nothing bad coming for you because of some action you've taken.

But what about "holy"? We sing the word in countless songs about God, but do we know what it means? Do we realize that holiness is something we must strive for?

Have you ever known someone who has a special set of dishes they only break out on special occasions? Probably everybody's grandmother has something like this. Antique plates and silverware that sit safe and secure all year long until the family comes over for Thanksgiving. You'll never see her eating dinner off of them on a regular night, because she reserves them for only the most special of occasions. They have been set apart from the rest of the dishes to be put to use only when it really counts.

In a similar way, something that is holy is *set apart* for use by God. It's something that's elevated a little bit above everything else because it doesn't serve ordinary purposes. We call the Bible holy because it isn't like the rest of the books you can put on a shelf. It's used specifically to draw people closer to God and to share His Word.

A pilgrim is a holy vessel. They live in the world, yes; they interact with the world, sure; but they have been given a special purpose and a special use. They are to draw people into a relationship with a God who is holy. He is set apart from the world, the same as His children are.

- **What does it mean to be set apart for use by God?**

- **Consider your life for a moment. Have you been set apart for use by God, or are you still concerned with worldly things?**

- **Journal a prayer to God asking Him to set you apart for His use.**

LIVING WITH EXCELLENCE

Look through your Bible to find 2 Peter 1:3-4 and Philippians 1:9-10. Both of these passages are concerned with something specific: *excellence*. We are to be excellent because God is excellent.

Excellence is about becoming or making the decision to continually aim at a standard that is pleasing to God. This does not contradict the reality that in Christ, God is already pleased with us. We don't aim to earn His favor; we aim to please and glorify Him because He has already shown us favor.

The highest good should always be the goal in the journey. We are to seek the highest good throughout the various dimensions of our lives—home, culture, vocation, church—because we seek to live a life Jesus can be proud of.

Once you practice this approach of pursuing excellence, you will begin to notice some changes. Changes like a low tolerance for mediocrity in your journey. Being average becomes something other people do, but not you. Achieving excellence gives you a taste for it you never even knew you could have. It's like when you start to eat healthy and discover you actually enjoy it. Then after months of eating food that's good for you, the idea of a fast food diet is a notion you just can't stomach! Excellence continually achieved is like maintaining a strict diet of the highest good.

And we pursue excellence because God modeled it for us first.

- **Take a few minutes to reflect on the excellence God modeled. Look around you at the things He made and the order He instilled into everything around you.**

- **Does your life reflect a pilgrim's life who is devoted to pursuing the kind of excellence God modeled?**

LIVING WITH SUBSTANCE

There is a very old story that takes place in a cave.

In this story, a person was born and grew up, never moving from the same spot. Every single day, he would wake up chained to a wall in a cave. He'd have food and water provided for him, but he never knew anything except the chains on his limbs. Interestingly, the only thing he could see was the wall directly in front of him.

Now, he could hear everything perfectly fine. If a camel walked behind him and cast a shadow on the wall, he would recognize the outline and hear the sounds a camel makes—the clopping of its hooves, the way it would shudder or sneeze every now and then. But as far as this man knew, camels were just humped, shadowy figures walking across the wall in front of him. The same went for people, or elephants, or trees. He only knew them by the way their shadows looked.

So one day, when he broke free, he discovered the world looked a lot different than he imagined it did. Things had depth and color, texture and smell. The substance had something different than the shadow did: it felt real. Alive. Breathing.

Sometimes it is tempting to fake purity or holiness or excellence. To put on a mask that looks like those things, but is actually empty underneath. May this never be said of pilgrims living for the cause of Christ. May it be said, instead, that we have been changed from the inside, that we are people of action and forward motion, that we dream big and accomplish big, all in a genuine, real way. We are people of substance, not just the shadows of it.

- **When have you seen someone who was faking being something they weren't?**

- **When have you been the faker?**

- **What can you do to be more genuine in your pilgrim's walk today?**

Session 7

10PM: SANCTIFYING FAILURE AND HOLY REGRET

Start by watching the video of Brent's teaching for Session 7. As you watch the video, complete the following:

List some potential sources of anxiety and stress in Paul's life that Brent mentioned.

-
-
-
-

What is on your list of things that cause you anxiety and stress?

-
-
-

How would Paul have dealt with failure and is all failure the same?

How can you keep your mistakes and past failures from hindering your progress in your pilgrim journey?

How can your failures be redeemed? How was this true of Paul?

How might God's grace in Christ reshape your view of your past? Your future?

The gospel changes everything. Past and even present failures no longer define the pilgrim journeying toward the heaven country. In today's session, we will see how a deep and abiding relationship with Jesus frees us from the guilt of the past and eases our anxiety about the future allowing us to live with holy purpose in the present.

One of the most difficult things to do is to look back on the things we regret. We want to push it out of our memory, to believe we're different now.

Take a few minutes to write a definition for "regret." When you're done, go around the room and share what you wrote.

What do your definitions have in common? How are they different?

If we were to ask the dictionary what "regret" is, it would tell us, "a feeling of sadness, repentance, or disappointment over an occurrence or something that one has done or failed to do."[1] We can regret all kinds of things: things we have done, things we should have done, things we could have done better. Even if we have learned from our mistakes, it's far too easy to get trapped in a cycle of regret.

What kinds of actions lead to feelings of regret for you?

Do you think it's possible to live a life without regret? Why or why not?

It's easy to look at Paul as a spiritual giant. He traveled most of the known world, planting churches everywhere he went and sending letters of encouragement to the places he couldn't reach. He encountered sick people and healed them through God's power; he encountered demons and cast them out in Jesus' name. He was beaten and imprisoned for his faith and never renounced it—instead, his faith grew stronger with every passing day.

But Paul wasn't always this way. As he came to the end of his journey, he probably found himself looking back on the years he spent believing Jesus to be a fake, a pretend Messiah. He might have remembered the people he imprisoned and had murdered because of their faith in Jesus. He might have even remembered the reputation he carried when he started following Jesus and the fear that came over Christians' eyes when he walked in a room.

How in the world could Paul overcome his enormous past failures? How could he live with the regret he might have felt for the person he used to be? Let's discover how to overcome the different kinds of failures you will inevitably face on your pilgrim's journey.

SIN IS FAILURE THAT DISPLEASES GOD

The moment you were born, you became a part of a system ruled by an overbearing master: Sin.

What is sin?

How can you know what sin is?

What effect does sin have on your relationship with God?

Sin is not some random selection from a long list of don'ts in the Bible. It is not just lust or murder. Sin is, at its core, rebellion against a perfect God. Whenever you place something other than God on the throne of your life, that is sin. You are worshiping self over God. It might look different—it could be taking something that doesn't belong to you, telling a lie, or any number of more serious things—but sin is sin in God's eyes. No matter how great or small. And we humans are very good at sinning. Let's look at three steps to overcoming failure.

STEP 1: WHEN ONE PERSON BELIEVES IN YOU

Look at what happened when Paul, a notorious sinner, was introduced to a man named Barnabas in Acts 9:

> When he [Saul/Paul] arrived in Jerusalem, he tried to join the disciples, but they were all afraid of him, since they did not believe he was a disciple. Barnabas, however, took him and brought him to the apostles and explained to them how Saul had seen the Lord on the road and that the Lord had talked to him, and how in Damascus he had spoken boldly in the name of Jesus (Acts 9:26-27).

Why would it have taken courage for Barnabas to stand up for Paul like that?

When is a time someone had your back and stood up for you even when others didn't?

One of the things that helps us overcome catastrophic failure is having someone in our corner believing we can be better than we have been. When we fall, we need someone to come alongside of us and, instead of getting angry that we fell, look past our failure and help us get back to our feet.

STEP 2: WHEN GOD'S GRACE IS LOUDER THAN OUR PAST SINS

Read aloud a few verses at a time from Paul's testimony in Acts 22:1-21.

What was Paul like before encountering Jesus?

How did he encounter Jesus?

How was he different afterward?

These three elements are the essence of any testimony of a life saved by Christ, and they all hinge around something miraculous: God's grace. God did not owe it to Paul to save him out of his sin, but He did it anyway. He gave Paul a gift he would spend the rest of his life being grateful for. He saved him.

STEP 3: WHEN YOUR FUTURE BECOMES MORE RELEVANT THAN YOUR PAST

It took a little bit of time, but before long, Paul wasn't just the ex-Pharisee that was radically saved. He became God's chosen instrument to be the great apostle to the Gentiles. It was his future, his calling.

Paul had been radically saved by grace, but still had to labor to win over the people who were (rightfully) skeptical of him. He found solace in a single, solitary person who believed in him and gave him a chance. He never forgot the grace which had freed him, and he labored for years to plant seeds of churches wherever he could, and then eventually began to see growth. It was a long process and was probably frustrating at times, but Paul never forgot that his future was more relevant than his past.

What has been the most difficult time in your life?

Whether it was a particularly difficult class or a strained relationship with a friend or family member, we've all had to overcome something before.

What kept you going during that difficult time?

How does keeping your eye on the future help you get through difficult times?

For Paul, understanding his calling and knowing where God was leading him helped him endure all kinds of struggles and, most importantly, overcome his difficult past. Only through the grace of God could a Pharisee breathing murderous threats against Christians become the most famous apostle in history.

All pilgrims are living a story and walking on a journey back home. Part of that story—the most important part of that story—is why they're journeying in the first place. Everyone who walks the Christian life does so from a position of grace. We were dead in our sins, but God raised us to life—a thing we could never earn, and a gift we could never repay.

Take a few minutes to write down a short version of your testimony like the one we read from Paul. Then practice sharing those stories with your group.

Who were you before Jesus saved you?

How did you encounter Jesus?

How have you been different since?

REGRET IS A PRISON OF OUR OWN MAKING

Because the past cannot be changed, the regret some people experience becomes a prison of guilt. When regret leads to guilt, we wallow away in the pile of bad decisions wondering if the lock will ever be taken off this prison of our own making.

Guilt can be such an impossible weight to shoulder. On the outside we may look like we are holding everything together, but on the inside we are like an abused child curled up in the corner of a dark room. That's the thing with guilt, it forces you to become two different people. If guilt were a theatrical performance, it would be a one-man show forcing you to play different parts.

People try to cope with guilt in so many different ways. Many seek to punish or numb themselves in hopes of alleviating their guilty consciences. These activities include everything from self-harm to extreme physical exercise, from substance abuse to becoming a workaholic. Some people throw themselves into a charity or some kind of service to others in an effort to work off the burden of guilt, like a debt that is owed. But if you have ever struggled with guilt—and we all have—then you know our best efforts can't remove the weight of it. That regret is still there, reminding us of our inadequacy and fueling the guilt all the more.

The good news for us is Jesus sets us free from this kind of regret. He died so our sins could be forgiven in God's eyes. He gives us a new purpose that supersedes the person we used to be. He instills a new heart in us to replace the stony, cracked one we had before knowing Him. We do not have to be imprisoned by our guilt anymore because Jesus makes us entirely new.

- **What is something you have trouble moving on from in your past?**

- **Have you asked Jesus to forgive you of your past and carry you away from it?**

- **How can you walk in freedom today knowing Christ has forgiven you?**

FEAR THAT HOLDS OUR FUTURE HOSTAGE

Fear can be just as destructive to our souls as guilt, especially when we let our fears hold our futures hostage. This happens when I regret something so much that fear and shame consume me, and I am unable to move forward. The idea of fear robbing us of our future is as old as time itself. In Genesis 3, Eve engaged the serpent in conversation, and both she and Adam ate the fruit of the tree God had told them not to eat. We then see the fall of mankind into sin. Adam and Eve rebelled against the clearly stated will of God when he said:

> You are free to eat from any tree of the garden, but you must not eat from the tree of the knowledge of good and evil, for on the day you eat from it, you will certainly die (Gen. 2:16-17).

Of course we know how the story goes. They both ate the fruit, and instead of having godlike power, their eyes were opened to their own inadequacy and shame. So they covered their nakedness with fig leaves and hid from God when he came walking in the garden. They were then forced to face the truth:

> So the LORD God called out to the man and said to him, "Where are you?" And he said, "I heard you in the garden, and I was afraid because I was naked, so I hid" (Gen. 3:9-10).

It's amazing to think that prior to this, Adam and Eve had never experienced fear. In fact, God only wanted them to experience good things from Him, and fear wasn't on the list. Fear was the result of realizing and regretting a decision they had made that was contrary to what God had asked. Maybe we should think about it this way—the emotion God didn't want us to experience was the first emotion we did experience after we failed to follow His guidance.

- **What are you fearful of when it comes to the future?**

- **How does walking as a pilgrim keep you from living in fear of the future?**

- **What fears do you need to turn over to the Lord today?**

FREEDOM THAT COMES FROM REDEMPTION

Regret can destroy our lives if we let it. But just as the story of Adam and Eve doesn't end with their rebellion, so our journeys don't have to end with our regrets. The hope of redemption first mentioned in the creation narrative (Gen. 3:15) is the only pathway to freedom from guilt and fear.

If you want freedom, you have to lay your regret at the feet of Jesus, repent of the past mistake that caused your regret, and repent for holding on to that regret and not living forgiven. Then, and only then, will we experience freedom. Freedom from regret, as a source of guilt and fear, happens when we actually believe God when he says:

> But now, apart from the law, the righteousness of God has been revealed, attested by the Law and the Prophets. The righteousness of God is through faith in Jesus Christ to all who believe, since there is no distinction. For all have sinned and fall short of the glory of God. They are justified freely by his grace through the redemption that is in Christ Jesus. (Rom. 3:21-24).

The gift of God's righteousness freely given to us by His grace is our only hope for freedom. It's as if we were slaves to our regrets, guilt, and fear, and He brought us out of slavery into freedom. He redeemed us by His blood.

When we believe we have been justified freely by His grace, then the option of living in guilt and fear is no longer available to us. We have been redeemed from the guilt and fear brought on by regrets, and they now simply serve as a memorial to God's grace in our lives. The cause of the regret can't be erased—it happened. But we can live forgiven and free. Regret now simply reminds us of the person we never want to be again. It reminds us of how we have been completely forgiven; it reminds us to live redeemed. It is no longer just regret, it is now a regret redeemed.

- **Describe the person you were before you met Christ.**

- **How did you meet Christ, and how did He change you? What does it mean to you that He redeemed you?**

- **How are you different now than you used to be?**

THE FUTURE IS MORE RELEVANT THAN THE PAST

Your past does not own you. Your past does not control your future. If you have been given life in Christ, all of that has been redeemed. And since it has been redeemed, you are now in a spectacular position: your future has become more relevant than your past.

Perhaps these weeks have been your first steps on your pilgrim's journey back home, or maybe they come somewhere in the middle. Whatever the case, the rest of your journey lies in front of you. You are walking on a road toward your heavenly home at the end of your journey.

Take stock of the things around you. Notice the people in your life, the activities you're involved in, the different circles of influence you have. Understand the things that give you anxiety, the things that cause you fear, and the things that give you hope. And then keep moving forward. As a pilgrim you are no longer bound by the stretch of road behind you. You are solely focused on where you are going, and the King you are walking toward.

In his letter to the Philippian church, Paul wrote, "I pursue as my goal the prize promised by God's heavenly call in Christ Jesus" (Phil. 3:14). This was the thing that kept Paul motivated. It commanded all of his attention. It helped him survive all of his hardships, overcome his tumultuous past, and focused all of his efforts while he was away from home.

Because heaven was his home. And he couldn't wait to get back.

- **How has your perspective of the Christian journey changed over the past seven weeks?**

- **How does understanding your heavenly home give you hope for the future?**

- **If you had to pick one thing right now, what do you feel the Lord calling you to do?**

- **How can you make sure you are walking in that direction from this day forward?**

Session 8

11PM: LIFE IMITATES STORY

Start by watching the video of Brent's teaching for Session 8. As you watch the videos, fill in the following blanks and answer the questions.

Who were the four audiences Jesus addressed from the cross?

-

-

-

-

God's _____ for my life is God's enduring _____ in my life.

What kind of story are you telling with your life? Who is the central figure or hero of the narrative that is your journey?

When you tell a story with your life that has redemption as its theme and the Redeemer as the hero, not only is your story worth _____, your story is worth _____.

The entire point of the pilgrimage is to _____ God.

While the end of our lives might seem a long way off, why is it important that we think carefully now about what it means to finish well?

As Paul's life drew to a close, he likely thought about the overall message the story of his life told. In this final session, therefore, we will consider what it means to finish well: to run the race of this life with integrity, purpose, and a desire to please God.

We have nearly reached the stroke of midnight.

Paul's long race has come to an end at last, his final moment approaching. All of the struggles he endured, all of the mistakes that had been redeemed, all of the lives he'd encountered and seen changed by the gospel—all of it is over for Paul, now.

It's difficult to think of this moment while we sit in our rooms, while we drive our cars, while we go about the busyness of our days. Some stay intentionally busy in order to block out the thought of our final moment. Some get brief glimpses of it and are paralyzed by the thought. Others are gripped with fear or anxiety.

But not Paul. Paul spent his last moments with no regrets, encouraging his spiritual son. Look at some of the things he wrote Timothy in this final hour:

> *For I am already being poured out as a drink offering, and the time for my departure is close (2 Tim. 4:6).*

> *I have fought the good fight, I have finished the race, I have kept the faith (2 Tim. 4:7).*

> *Make every effort to come to me soon (2 Tim. 4:9).*

Judging by these three verses, what do you think Paul was feeling?

What words or phrases make you think that?

Do you think Paul's attitude toward dying is similar or different from most people's? Why or why not?

As Paul was being led to his death, moments away from entering the heaven country, he resorted back to a source of strength upon which he had relied for most of his life: Jesus Christ. Undoubtedly, he would have been comforted reflecting on the way Jesus had died all those years ago.

What better example was there to follow as he prepared to finally go home? After all, Jesus did something remarkable that would have comforted Paul in these final moments: He taught us how to die well.

JESUS DIED EXTENDING GRACE TO THE UNDESERVING

Something everybody loves in movies is when the bad guy finally gets what's coming to him once the hero tracks him down. After an entire movie's worth of the bad guy getting away with his evil deeds, we cheer once the main character has his last hurrah and exacts the payback we've been waiting for.

What's your favorite movie in which the bad guy finally gets what's coming to him?

Why do you think the bad guy got what he deserved?

Jesus lived His very own version of this kind of story. He was hanging from splintery wood, still bleeding and raw from beatings, still humiliated from the insults and the nakedness, still reeling from having been betrayed by a close friend, denied by another, and deserted by most of the rest. He was a man wrongfully convicted and wrongfully punished—and if this had been a Hollywood production, He would have found a way to suddenly, miraculously, exact vengeance on all of the people who had put Him there.

But He didn't. Instead, He did something even more miraculous. He showed them grace.

Look at what He said in Luke 23:34: "Father, forgive them, because they do not know what they are doing."

Forgive them? How in the world could they be forgiven? How could He even ask for that?

Because Jesus was showing us that forgiveness can never be understood apart from sacrifice—and no one can grant forgiveness from sin but God alone. Jesus knew that the forgiveness He wanted to give, even to the people who had hurt Him the most, could not come unless He died for them.

How does Jesus' sacrifice for you change the way you see yourself?

What should your life look like knowing that your sin has been forgiven and what you really deserve is punishment?

Paul most definitely took a cue from Jesus, because he did something amazing toward the end of his letter to Timothy:

At my first defense, no one stood by me, but everyone deserted me. May it not be counted against them (2 Tim. 4:16).

They'd abandoned Paul in his hour of need, but still he didn't hold it against them. He forgave them even when he had nothing to gain from it, and even though they did not deserve it.

Who is someone who has wronged you? Maybe they deserted you, or maybe they hurt you. Maybe they spread rumors about you or went out of their way to embarrass you.

What might it look like for you to forgive that person?

Paul knew that here, on his last leg, holding grudges or counting offenses against him was as pointless as it was when he was young and healthy. He valued reconciliation over being bitter, even when he was in the right and they were in the wrong.

I think Paul was telling Timothy the exact same thing he'd told the church at Corinth a few years before this: "Imitate me, as I also imitate Christ" (1 Cor. 11:1).

If you told someone to imitate you, what kind of life would they be living?

If you told someone to imitate you, what kinds of thoughts would they have about the people around them?

If you told someone to imitate you, how would they treat their family and those closest to them?

Paul gave us something amazing: an example of the Christian life. He showed us how to live and die in a way that glorifies God. His pilgrimage had come to an end, but a greater story was just beginning. Paul had finished … Paul would now begin. And therein lies the glorious outcome for all pilgrims wandering their way homeward—when we finish, it's really just the beginning.

As you go on your way as a pilgrim journeying back home, consider the lessons we've learned from Paul in his final hours. Dress with grace and put on the life of Christ. Live a life worth telling stories about and worth imitating—because if people hear and imitate you, it will bring them straight to Jesus' feet.

Leader
GUIDE

Dear Leaders,

Thank you for committing to teaching your students to make the most of the time God has given them by examining the apostle Paul's life of gospel impact. It is our hope and prayer that God will use this study to draw students into a deeper relationship with Jesus and move them to joyfully and passionately embrace their own journeys' toward heaven that Christ has laid before them. In hopes of helping you do this, we have prepared a Leader Guide for each of the eight sessions.

Here is a brief explanation of each section of the Leader Guide and how to use it:

MAIN POINT: This statement makes clear the central truth you'll be teaching and driving home to students each week.

KEY SCRIPTURE REFERENCES: The primary passages of Scripture covered in each session are listed here, so you might read and meditate on them in preparation for leading each session.

OPTIONAL ICE BREAKER: Consider using the optional activity described in this section to begin your time together and get students engaged and participating in group discussion.

KEY POINTS OUTLINE: Here you will find a basic outline of what you will be covering in each session. Review these points prior to each session and take note of which points will be most important for you to focus on this week.

PRAYER PROMPT: This section offers some direction on how to pray for yourself and your students in light of the teaching of each session.

FOLLOW UP: Your students' pilgrim journeys are just beginning. This section encourages you to connect with them during the week following each session as a means of encouraging them to put into practice what they've learned.

Week 1

MAIN POINT:
The Christian life is a journey, and we are pilgrims. What story would you like your life to tell?

KEY SCRIPTURE REFERENCES: Hebrews 11:1-12

OPTIONAL ICE BREAKER:
Speed Friending. Create two groups of students. Have one group sit in stations around the room, and have the other group rotate one station to the right every time you tell them to switch. Provide a few questions for them to discuss, such as: What's your name? What kind of movies do you enjoy? What sports do you play?

After about a minute, tell the rotating group to move to the next station, and repeat until they return to their original positions. You are all about to embark on a journey together; you should get to know one another a little better.

KEY POINTS OUTLINE:
- Every believer is a pilgrim, a representative of heaven, on a journey back home.
- A pilgrim understands that his or her life is all about a journey.
- A pilgrim is willing to exhaust his or her resources to journey well.
- A pilgrim believes one journey can change the world.
- A pilgrim understands the road is difficult, but the destination is worth it.
- You get to decide what kind of story your life will tell.

PRAYER PROMPT:
Pray for wisdom and endurance as we embark on this eight-week journey together. Pray that Jesus makes Himself known at every turn.

FOLLOW-UP SUGGESTIONS:
Text or email your group with encouragement throughout the week to be diligent in remaining in the Word.

NOTES:

Week 2

MAIN POINT:
Pilgrims are not meant to walk alone. As we journey alongside other believers, let's learn how to be the kinds of companions each other needs.

KEY SCRIPTURE REFERENCES: 2 Timothy 1:4; 4:11-12

OPTIONAL ICE BREAKER:
Name That Person. Divide the group into two teams, and pass out note cards and pens. Ask everyone to write down two or three things about themselves on their card they don't think anyone else would know. Shuffle the cards and have each group try to guess which person on the other team wrote which card. The team that gets the most correct wins.

Pilgrims should strive to see and understand each other. This will help teach your group to look past the surface of what they see in their fellow pilgrims.

KEY POINTS OUTLINE:
- We were built for companionship and friendship.
- True friends prioritize presence over productivity—being there for each other is important.
- True friends don't have to qualify to receive quality—friends give their best even when it's difficult.
- True friends seek to understand before being understood.

PRAYER PROMPT:
Pray for the strength to be a good friend to the people your group listed. Ask that Jesus be shown in every one of their actions.

FOLLOW-UP SUGGESTIONS:
Check in to see how the people in your group are following through with their action plan to be a better, truer friend to the person they listed.

NOTES:

Week 3

MAIN POINT:

The Wardrobe of Grace is the outfit pilgrims put on if they want to be appropriately dressed.

KEY SCRIPTURE REFERENCES: Colossians 3:12-14; Proverbs 15:1; John 8:6-11; Matthew 11:28-30

OPTIONAL ICE BREAKER:

Last week, we talked all about friendship. Go around the room and ask your group to describe their friend and what they did to be a better friend to them last week.

KEY POINTS OUTLINE

- The "Wardrobe of Grace" from Colossians 3:12-14
  - Kindness: How we relate to others
  - Humility: How we view ourselves
  - Gentleness: Our attitude toward others
- The daily devotionals help us explore the rest of the articles. Wear them well!

PRAYER PROMPT:

Pray for God to outfit you with the Wardrobe of Grace, so you can be appropriately dressed to handle what life throws at you, and so the people looking in at your life can see Christ in the way you treat them.

FOLLOW-UP SUGGESTIONS:

Encourage students to be diligent in their devotionals, because this week they are exploring the other four articles in the Wardrobe of Grace on their own.

NOTES:

Week 4

MAIN POINT:

Pilgrims walking together have enough trying to tear them apart. We should be known, instead, for our radical unity.

KEY SCRIPTURE REFERENCES: Romans 1:7; Acts 2:42-46

OPTIONAL ICE BREAKER:

As your group arrives, have each of them write their name on a slip of paper. When everyone is present, pass out a sheet of paper and a pencil to everyone in your group, and have them draw one of the names out of a hat. They are to draw a picture of the person whose name they pulled from the hat. Collect the drawings and see if the group can guess who was drawn! As we learn to practice unity, sometimes that starts with just seeing each other accurately. Even if we can't draw very well, we can take time to observe and notice things about each other.

KEY POINTS OUTLINE:

- There are a lot of forces in this world trying to divide believers. So we should have:
  - One Mind: Unity of will
  - One Mission: Unity is a team sport
  - One Outcome: A common goal
- Identify points of disunity and endeavor to change them.

PRAYER PROMPT:

Pray for the kind of unity that only Christ can bring. Ask God to help you grow closer to each other and closer to Him, and for the wisdom to be able to see through the things that don't matter and focus on the things that do.

FOLLOW-UP SUGGESTIONS:

Now that your group is growing closer together, you may think about planning some kind of get-together outside of group time. Plan a fun evening to help your group grow together in unity.

NOTES:

Week 5

MAIN POINT:
God accomplishes His will, even if it seems impossible, through His people.

KEY SCRIPTURE REFERENCES: Romans 12:4-8; 1 Thessalonians 5:15-22;
1 Corinthians 10:31

OPTIONAL ICE BREAKER:
The lesson begins by looking at the numerous ways the world tries to divide us. So begin by asking your students, "Sometimes it feels like the world is going crazy. If you could offer up one solution to fixing the world's craziness—that would bring everyone together—what would it be?"

KEY POINTS OUTLINE:
- Pilgrims are a new breed of thinkers. They have several things that set them apart:
  - Unshakable belief
  - Sacred gifting
  - Unwavering focus
- We are to use what we have in order to bring God glory.

PRAYER PROMPT:
Pray for God to reveal the ways he has gifted you, personally. Then, pray for opportunities to use that gifting to bring Him glory.

FOLLOW-UP SUGGESTIONS:
Encourage your group as they refocus their eyes on Christ and wake up every day ready to look to Him alone.

NOTES:

Week 6

MAIN POINT:
Whatever you eat, whatever you drink, whatever you do, it should all be done excellently, for the glory of God.

KEY SCRIPTURE REFERENCES: 2 Timothy 2:15; Philippians 1:9-10; 4:8; Colossians 3:23

OPTIONAL ICE BREAKER:
Have your group sit in a circle and go around, saying, "Hello. My name is _____, and I am ___% here today." Then, give your students a chance to get off their chest something bothering or distracting them from being fully present in the group. You might lead by example, showing them it is okay to be honest with each other.

Living a life of excellence requires focus, and sometimes to be focused we have to acknowledge the different directions our attention is being pulled.

KEY POINTS OUTLINE:
- God has modeled excellence for us.
- Excellence is a decision and an achievement.
- Excellence is substance over shadow.
- Leave your group with a charge to be excellent and an encouragement to dive deeper into the ideas you touched on in group time during their devotionals this week.

PRAYER PROMPT:
Thank God for demonstrating excellence, and pray for the focus and strength to practice it every day.

FOLLOW-UP SUGGESTIONS:
This week, students are going to be diving more in-depth into some of the things you addressed as a group. Encourage them to personalize what they learn so they can practice excellence in every aspect of their lives.

NOTES:

Week 7

MAIN POINT:

Most of us live with regrets in our past. But our past selves have been redeemed and paid for by Jesus. That frees us up to look forward to where God is leading us.

KEY SCRIPTURE REFERENCES: Acts 22:1-21

OPTIONAL ICE BREAKER:

We're going to be talking about failure and regret this week. But you don't have to start out heavy. Instead, go around and ask your group, "When was a time, as a child, that you got in trouble with your parents?"

KEY POINTS OUTLINE:

- Sin is failure that displeases God. But failure can be overcome.
- We can overcome failure and help our brothers and sisters overcome failure by believing in one another.
- We can overcome failure by understanding that God's grace is louder than our past sins.
- We can overcome failure by seeing that our future is more relevant than our past.
- Encourage your group to think about and verbalize their testimonies, as laid out in the final exercise.

PRAYER PROMPT:

Thank the Lord for His sacrifice on your behalf and for making you new. Lay down your failures and regrets at His feet, ask forgiveness for your sins, and pray for Him to guide you steadily forward.

FOLLOW-UP SUGGESTIONS:

Your group is going to be looking within this week. Encourage them to do it seriously and to deepen their understanding of what Jesus did for them and how they should respond to it.

NOTES:

Week 8

MAIN POINT:
Even though Paul could have lamented his coming death, he didn't. He died how Jesus died: extending grace to those who didn't deserve it.

KEY SCRIPTURE REFERENCES: Luke 23:34; 2 Timothy 4:16; 1 Corinthians 11:1

OPTIONAL ICE BREAKER:
Go around the room and ask each student to list one thing he or she learned over the last eight weeks that someone else would benefit from learning or hearing.

KEY POINTS OUTLINE:
- Paul could have lamented his final hours, but he didn't. Instead, he followed Jesus' model for how to die well.
- Jesus extended grace to the undeserving.
- Paul extended grace, also.
- Paul implored Timothy to follow his example, because he was following Christ's.

PRAYER PROMPT:
Pray that the things we've learned from Paul's life would stick, and that we could live lives worthy of the gospel—and worthy of being imitated.

FOLLOW-UP SUGGESTIONS:
The final week is not the end, but the beginning. As you wrap up your two months together, you can now put what you've learned from studying Paul's life into practice. Encourage them to live a life that would allow them to tell someone, as Paul did, "Imitate me, as I imitate Christ."

NOTES:

Sources

SESSION 1

1. F. Scott Fitzgerald, *The Great Gatsby* (New York: Scribner, 2003) 10.

SESSION 2

1. Kenneth S. Wuest, *Word Studies in the Greek New Testament, Vol. 3* (Grand Rapids, MI: Eerdmans Publishing, 1989), 2 Timothy 4:10.

2. C.S. Lewis, *Four Loves* (New York: Harcourt, 1988), 77.

3. "Benghazi Timeline: How the Attack Unfolded," *CBS News* [online], 13 May 2013, [accessed 25 August 2018]. Available from the Internet: https://www.cbsnews.com/news/benghazi-timeline-how-the-attack-unfolded/.

SESSION 4

1. A.T. Robertson, *Word Pictures in the New Testament* (Nashville: Broadman Press, 1933), Philippians 1:28.

SESSION 6

1. Andreas J. Kostenberger, *Excellence* (Wheaton: Crossway, 2011), 33.

SESSION 7

1. 'regret,' *Oxford Living Dictionary* (New York: Oxford University Press, 2018).

Notes